The American College Girl

THE AMERICAN COLLEGE GIRL

by K. C. Cirtautas

The Citadel Press   New York

Permission has been granted for quotations from *The Education of Women—Signs for the Future*, Opal D. David, ed., American Council on Education; *Educating Our Daughters* by Lynn White, Jr., Harper & Brothers; *Achievement in the College Years. A Record of Intellectual and Personal Growth*, Lois B. Murphy and Esther Rauschenbusch, eds., Harper & Brothers; *They Went to College* by Ernest Havemann and Patricia Salter West, copyright, 1952, by Time, Inc. Reprinted by permission of Harcourt, Brace & World, Inc.; *A Century of Higher Education for American Women* by Mabel Newcomer, copyright, 1959, by Mabel Newcomer, Harper & Brothers; "Smith: A College for ARG's with High IQ's" by David Boroff, March 1961 issue of *Mademoiselle*, copyright, 1961, by Street & Smith Publications, Inc., by permission of the author.

378
C492

44238
Dec. 1962

FIRST EDITION

To all those who are looking
for delicate subtle points in
human behavior and endeavor

Contents

Foreword

Any hardened schoolman who dips into this book is likely at first to surmise that its author is what used to be called an "old softie." The college girl to whom one is introduced is akin to her whom the poet Crashaw once enthusiastically described as "the not impossible she." Though she plays games, sits on a rock dangling her feet, drinks a coke in the lounge, lights a cigarette and puts through a call to her boy friend, she remains none the less a gracious creature who moves sedately through a world of books, teachers, campus lawns, flowers, and skiing in the wintertime. And our schoolman may rub his eyes again and wonder what has happened to all the girls who brood over broken homes, suffer from incurable love outlasting every phase of the moon, fail in classes, or strut about with boys' shirts dangling above ridiculous slacks.

But being myself about as hardened as anyone is likely to be who has presided for a long time over the destiny of college women milling in and out of generations, I was in the end persuaded that our author is quite right. Perhaps no one except a man with a European background could manage to judge this part of the American scene so wisely and rightly. For, after all, the American college girl is the princess in the fabulous society which, by reason of a kind Providence, we have been able to devise if not complete. This sociey provides the most widespread emancipation from physical drudgery, and the most breathtaking commitment to intellectual pursuits history has ever known. To think that a hundred years ago Vassar had not yet opened its gates, and that generally even the daughters of prosperous families did little with their minds except steep them in a thimbleful of piano music and the verse of Godey's *Lady's Book*! Now there are thousands upon thousands of girl students on campuses big and little, and more would come if they could. It is a scene which wipes out many differences between the wealthy and the poor, and sometimes those which separate the races.

These girls are a serious lot, by and large. They have to be because otherwise the colleges make room for others. While few of them—unfortunately very few, indeed—will go on to lead scholarly lives, most will have ranged far over the "golden pastures" of knowledge and sometimes even have heard Triton and his horn. Youth is in their bones, of course, and youth is supple, charming, often very beautiful. Nor is it merely youngness of the body. Of course this book does not capture the radiance of young moods, emotions, loyalties and ideas as poetically as does Meredith's *Ordeal of Richard Feverel*, for example. But for once we have here a teacher who does not run away from it but stops to listen, share and love. Why should one always pass this ever-changing yet gloriously constant panorama by? There is more to the story by far than pretty heads into which calculus or history is being pumped. And because what our author says about it comes out of an affection so genuine and so wholly without dross, there can be no doubt that many will like the book very much and turn for once to contemplation of the marvels of our common life rather than to any sort of clinical dissection of what is wrong with it.

GEORGE N. SHUSTER

Author's Preface

Large or small, sectarian or non-sectarian, exclusive or less exclusive, located in the East or in the West, the *basic patterns* are the same or almost the same everywhere in American institutions of higher education and learning. My interest is centered primarily on the resident student of a women's college and is carried out with an eye toward the details and nuances of these basic patterns.

In this study, I present the American college girl as I saw her during my ten years with her either as her teacher or as one who happened to meet her by choice or by chance. As a teacher, I had her at College Misericordia for five years and at Newton College of the Sacret Heart for three years; as a Research Fellow at Harvard, I became acquainted with many students from Radcliffe, Wellesley, Smith, and Mount Holyoke; as a visitor, I conversed with her at Trinity in Washington, at Hunter in New York, and at Marywood in Scranton; as a traveler, I met her in trains and buses, in the air and on the sea. She came from Alabama and Arkansas, from California and Colorado, from Delaware and Georgia, from Kentucky and Missouri, from Virginia and Wisconsin. I encountered her window-shopping on Fifth Avenue in Manhattan, trying her French in Quebec, eating sandwiches at a railroad station in London, swimming in the Koenigssee and peering at the Mona Lisa in the Louvre.

In the classroom and in the library, in the dining hall and on the athletic field, at home and on the street, at prayer, at dances, in my conversations with her, in her conversations with others in the same group, in all the phases of her life to which I have had access, I have observed her conduct—I use this word in its broadest sense—in order to draw this picture of her. I have also used her letters and diaries insofar as they were available to me.

The present study is closely related to my book on the homeless individual, *The Refugee*,[1] which deals with the life of suffering. *The American College Girl* represents the life of joy. These two works are an attempt to interpret the chief characteristics of human life.

I should like to thank Sister Mary Denise, R.S.M., Dr. George N. Shuster, Mrs. Frieda Schutze, and last but not least my wife and my students at College Misericordia for their kind assistance in preparing the manuscript for publication.

K. C. C.

The American College Girl

On the Way to College

"I wish to come to Mills to be with horses."

Higher education for women is at present highly valued in the United States, and indications are that its importance will increase from year to year. The reason for this lies in the growing realization that higher education contributes to greater happiness. The foremost wish of the American girl is to enjoy life meaningfully and to partake of civilized prosperity. Today many girls all over the world cherish the same wish. In the case of an American girl, this wish is usually fulfilled, whereas among her contemporaries in many other countries it often remains unfulfilled.

What is the reason for this?

Every young American girl has the opportunity to obtain a higher education, and this is perhaps the most precious heritage of the truly democratic system of American education. An American girl, even one who comes from a family without means, can, if she is willing and intelligent, continue studying until she has reached her doctorate, and then go on to a good position. In other countries, ambitious and intelligent daughters of poor families usually do not attain this goal. There, people say: "If you are born poor, you will die poor." But this is not true in the United States.

Thus it is not surprising that the term "college" becomes familiar, very early, to the American high school girl.[2] She knows that a college or university is an institution of higher learning where, after finishing high school, she may study four years and obtain her bachelor's degree, her first academic degree. Furthermore, she knows that you can learn almost everything here, from chemistry to the art of cooking. She also knows that a college campus is a place where one is educated to a certain refinement and where one can educate oneself. But she knows, too, that you must work more seriously here than you did before, that you make your own decisions here and have more responsibility because you are more independent. Finally, she realizes that college is more expensive than high school study.

The American high school graduate can choose her future alma mater from among 158 colleges for girls and 456 coeducational colleges. These comprise institutions both large and small, private and state-owned, secular and religious, famous and less well known, rich and unendowed, old and new. Each of these institutions of higher learning has its own aims and its own character—distinctions which are already implied in the printed entrance requirements. One college, for example, will require a better-than-average intelligence on the part of the applicant, another will emphasize a talent for leadership, still others feel that a pleasing personality is a necessary criterion. There are also colleges that lay stress on whether or not the applicant is pretty.[3] Besides schools which are primarily interested in applicants from wealthy and socially prominent families, there are also those willing to accept young girls from families without means or social standing.

After careful investigation the applicant will also discover specific differences. For instance, the scholastic requirements are not the same in all colleges and are not equally strict. One college will dismiss a student at the end of her first year if she has not maintained the required average grade. Another will give her a second chance. Moreover, she will find that in one college a certain department, for example, music, will be better than in another. One college offers many opportunities for social life, whereas another is limited in this respect. One permits a girl to appear in shorts, even in class, and to smoke almost everywhere, even in bedrooms; in another, shorts may not be worn in public and smoking is permitted only in a special room and at special times. One campus is stricter about male visitors than another. College A has a swimming pool and riding horses[4]; college B has neither.

Thus every high school graduate who is intelligent, ambitious and has a good character can choose the place for her higher education and training according to her taste and her means, and can there become a college girl. About one-third of all American college students are girls. Some are resident students in girls' colleges. They belong to the élite of American society. They take an active part in the social and cultural changes which are going on in the New World. During their college days they live in a happy, intellectual atmosphere which animates and refreshes even the remotest regions of the country.

A young woman who goes to college distinguishes herself in this endeavor. She likes to experience life by living it on her own wisely, and by trying and doing things intelligently. All this is done in order to get a delight from saying, "*I* know," pointed out by Robert Frost in "A Girl's Garden." Here, she is growing in an admirable milieu; here, she becomes striking in a pleasant way.

Getting Acquainted With the Campus

Here, by all available means, she becomes committed to beauty which charms her so that she herself develops into a charming figure.

It is a place of many buildings, large and small, old and new, modern and less modern. But despite their differences, they comprise a unit. Usually they are situated on the outskirts of the city, far from all main traffic. Untouched by the noise of factories, by the dust of streets, by the commotion of business, they rise up serene and majestic. In the modern world harassed by mundane passions, they represent a small sheltered world which is dignified and calm.

If you enter this undisturbed little world, a world apart, you will find yourself first of all on broad, clean avenues shaded by large trees. If you are walking or driving you will instinctively slow down, refreshed by this new air. Your eye will be greeted by gay flowers, by carefully tended grounds to look at and to play on, by statues of men and women who have achieved something extraordinary in science and art, and you will become thoughtful.

Each building has a name. It is usually one that belonged to a person who made a distinct contribution to this little world, either spiritually or materially. You feel respect and gratitude toward someone who has given of his talents and powers for such a worthy cause. "Did the silent immortal realize that he contributed to the improvement of America and to the betterment of the world?" you reflect as you look down from the terrace of "his" building to the vastness of the sea, the loftiness of mountains or the hush of forests. Buildings, grounds, walks, athletic field—the whole campus is entrusted to the busy hands of faithful servants. They are here to keep orderly this little world dedicated to the spirit. Orderly in this case means: clean, beautiful, pleasant; it means stimulating to the mind, nourishing to the spirit, open to truth. All of them, from the president down to the cook in the kitchen, are chosen to serve a noble cause, to create an academic atmosphere in which the student can achieve harmonious growth. The material and spiritual levels of this particular world reach heights of simplicity, cleanliness, and beauty, and reflect the democratic spirit, the search for truth and joy.

The style of the buildings is simple, as is the design of the grounds, the line of the walks and the layout of the athletic fields. The appearance and conduct of the members of this community are likewise simple. The whole campus reflects a matter-of-factness which is not cold. Accents of warmth and comfort offset the purely prosaic in the picture and make it intimate, even endearing. Wherever one looks, one encounters a detail that gives the whole an enchanting appearance which inevitably makes a deep impression on the beholder—a small tree that is not lonely at the end of an avenue, a much admired rose on a hedge beside the hockey field, a sharpened pencil that someone has lost in the parking lot, a statue in the corridor which perhaps depicts a scene from the life of Beatrice, a classroom portrait of a scholar, the bright face of a smiling student on the steps, or an intelligent, friendly look from a passing professor. All these small, even insignificant details, without pretence or extravagance, enrich the atmosphere of this little world.

The simple, clear picture of the campus on which unpretentious houses, cultivated gardens, charming parks and beautiful views attract the human eye has another characteristic: its cleanliness and orderliness. A campus is one of the few places in the United States which is so conspicuously clean. This may be seen on the walks, in the halls, in the classroom,—everywhere. The campus always looks like a place that has just been put in order for a respected guest. Actually it is the American college girl herself who is her own guest on the clipped paths and neat terraces, in the clean classrooms and bright halls. She is always pleased at this cleanliness, she and all who are close to her.

Thus the emphasis in the college is on cleanliness and order. The college knows that in a clean environment living will be happier, more beautiful, more meaningful. Beyond that, it knows that cleanliness in the outer surroundings nurtures purity of the spirit within. In such an ordered environment life has a better chance to achieve beauty and truth. This impressive campus cleanliness is kept alive by the mutual effort of custodians and students. When a girl comes to college to live and study, she finds everything neat and clean. She quickly observes this and has the understanding, indeed, the willingness—which is very important—to maintain it, to live happily in an immaculate little world which shall be truly her own. She knows she must not throw scraps of paper around carelessly, drop cigarette ashes on the floor, leave orange peels lying on the terrace. She must not walk into rooms with mud on her shoes, wear a soiled dress one more time, or leave wilted flowers in her room. She must not touch books with fingers that are dirty, hand in work with spots and corrections, use words which are regarded as unclean. If a girl was more or less negligent before she became a citizen of the campus community, she will easily learn the wisdom of a clean life here. It is taught to her almost unconsciously. She learns it not so much by formal instruction on the part of the staff as by quiet observation of her older fellow-students, many of whom are so very much at home in matters of cleanliness that they teach her by mere example, without words. Keeping herself clean and cherishing cleanliness gradually becomes a habit and a taste which she accepts as a precious heritage of the better life. Later she will pass it on to others, inadvertently, in her behavior.

A Swiss woman who was guest instructor for a year in one of the girls' colleges of the United States said: "If the majority of American women could be educated in a girls' college, America would be the cleanest country on earth."

Simplicity and cleanliness are the basic elements of beauty, for a thing that is simple and clean is usually also felt to be beautiful. Beauty on the campus is revealed, moreover, in colorful nuances, and lends a deeper glow to objects and to persons in themselves pure and orderly. Beauty is the soul of the campus.

The fresh green of carefully trimmed grass on the lawns, walks lined with a pleasing variety of trees, gay flowers in the flower borders, on the terraces, in the corridors, in guest rooms and living rooms, nourish the spirit. Pictures, large and small, of ancient and modern classical subjects hang in the corridors of the buildings, in the reception rooms, in the library, in study halls. Their very presence contributes to the spirit of the campus, even if one does not pause to examine them thoughtfully. Here are all kinds of statues honoring the great men of religion, art and science. They are a constant source of stimulation, and awaken a striving for the things which are beautiful and imperishable.

But the beautiful terraces and gardens, trees and flowers, the beautiful pictures and monuments require a girl who is beautiful—a college girl. She is beautiful, not by the standards of a beauty queen, but because she is simple, clean, decent.

Everyone she meets, whether it be the president of the college or the janitor of the buildings, she greets with a courteous "Good morning," "Good afternoon," or "Good evening." Or she simply smiles or waves, naturally, as a child would. This is beautiful.

You do not see her with a wry face, with unshined shoes, with curlers in her hair. In this respect she is agreeably different from her contemporaries outside the campus. Her voice is soft and controlled, her laughter modulated, her conversation spiced with humor. If she occasionally gets excited and says or does something that goes beyond the limits of good taste, she quickly apologizes with an almost tremulous "I'm sorry." In this way she recovers the spiritual equilibrium which guides her conduct.

For relaxation she goes to the lounge, drinks a bottle of coke or smokes a cigarette, half reclining in a soft armchair. Or she slips into shorts, stretches out on her bed, or takes her ease in a lounge chair on the balcony of her dormitory.

Thus the college girl grows up in an environment that is simple and beautiful. But in the small, cultivated campus world she also breathes the air of pure democracy. This is another characteristic that gives the American girls' college splendor and dignity. In this respect a college is essentially different from a European private girls' school where, generally, only the daughters of wealth and aristocracy may enjoy life in an atmosphere of security and luxury. The American college is different. Not birth and money, but character and intelligence determine whether a girl is accepted and whether she remains in college. The daughter of a factory worker is treated exactly like the daughter of a corporation president. Both take the same paths to the classroom, swim in the same pool, go to the same dances, and perhaps even live in the same room.

Here a girl's standing is not as a rule judged by her parents' social position, but on the basis of what she may accomplish ethically and intellectually, how she adjusts to the new situation presented by the academic world.

This system, called forth in the service of the mind, is an excellent discipline in itself. Here we clearly realize that, besides an aristocracy of birth and wealth, there is another, nobler kind—the aristocracy of the mind. Wealth does not help much here, and poverty does not prevent a girl from successfully maintaining her position among the academic élite. On the contrary, we know from practical life that wealth is sometimes an obstacle, whereas poverty can be favorable to intellectual success.

Both the rich student and the one from a poor family discover something novel in their very first year. The first realizes that even though her father is famous, though he has a respected position and a great deal of money, her name will not automatically appear on the dean's list. The other discovers that she cannot be prevented from becoming an honor student because her father is unknown and has little money. This realization makes both girls thoughtful and throws them on their own resources. It helps to awaken them, to develop them and win them over to the service of the mind. This realization also brings with it a great responsibility which unites them and all the other students.

On the campus truth is sought for and probed. The whole atmosphere is such that the path to spiritual values along which searching students are led is pleasant and promising. Here we find warmth, kindliness and a friendly approach offered in an atmosphere of discriminating taste. In this spirit the girl is guided toward the better life.

The roses in the garden, the employees in their offices, the professors in classrooms and laboratories are there to awaken in the student a love for beauty and truth, to reveal to her values which transform human life into a thing of enduring joy. Here she learns not only the techniques which will later provide a good living for her, but also—indirectly, rather than directly—how to live more beautifully and joyfully. This is perhaps decisive. For the girl, as for the woman, it is important to have cultivated, discriminating taste, to be capable of gleaning the beautiful from every situation of life, and, so to speak, to be a sorceress who lightly transforms dark moments into radiant ones.

The art of beautiful living is practiced on the campus. Here the student is to become an artist of life, living in joy and for joy, not only for herself but for others as well.

The situation and the atmosphere on the campus are unusual, intended and planned for an unusual girl who, in tranquility and comfort, will enjoy this happiness for four years. Joy springs from her diligent search for knowledge and wisdom, for the truth which blesses. Here the substance of the unusual is the quality characterized by discrimination and high-mindedness. The American girls' college is the place where the student, in a pleasant manner most sympathetic to her nature, climbs from ignorance toward knowledge, from darkness toward light, in order to fulfill her destiny. Here, by all available means, she becomes committed to beauty which charms her so that she herself develops into a charming figure.

Many persons both at home and abroad are becoming more and more conscious of the growing light of beauty toward which the college girl joyfully moves. This awareness comes to them from the college girl herself who, wrapped in an aura of beauty, gives herself in beauty to others. Thus the life of her fellowmen achieves a new dignity, and to the careworn she gives a new sense of joy. In her presence even inanimate things appear more beautiful and more desirable.

From all this we can see the value of the girl living and studying on the campus—a value which is daily becoming more appreciated at home and in the world at large. This makes meaningful the expression which is heard far and wide: "the American college girl."

What is commonly known about the American college girl is that she is young. She enters college at seventeen or eighteen and leaves it at twenty-one or twenty-two. She dresses better, behaves better, is better informed and is able to marry a better man or achieve a better position in life. She also has better taste: she has a better vocabulary, a wider range of interests, and a surer taste, all of which she can employ as the means toward a better life.

The college girl is better. Better than whom? She is better than those who have never had a chance to learn, laugh and dream on a campus for four years. She is better than others who never struggled four years for a better physical and intellectual harmony in that dignified atmosphere which can probably be found only in an American girls' college. To become better, she will have to struggle for an enlightened mind, an enriched soul and cultivated looks—the sources of perpetual beauty which is visible in a "pure smile," incarnated in Leonardo's Mona Lisa and expressed by Valéry.

The task of the present essay is to show what it is that makes the American college girl seem better and to analyze this quality in all its aspects.

The Environment

*Often it seems to her that her world consists
of books and nothing else.*

There is plenty of space on a campus. It is not
monotonous. The large space is divided into several
smaller spaces, each of which differs from the other, being
planned for a different purpose. In this variety lies the
charm of the large campus space where the college girl
moves lithely from one building to another. It is a diversi-
fied space where she always finds something to do which
gratifies and enriches her daily life.

There is her room which is simply and comfortably
furnished. Here she lives; that is to say, she studies and
sleeps here. She creates an atmosphere in her room which
makes it possible for her to study more easily, to sleep
more soundly and to dream more happily. The colors of
the things she has brought with her help to achieve this,
as well as the intimate furnishings and accessories arranged according to her own plan and taste, and the pictures on the walls, chosen according to the dictates of her

fancy and her longing. This room also reflects the enthusiasm of her young heart to be a model college girl.

She has books everywhere—on her desk, on shelves, on
the floor. Here in her room she must seriously cope with
voluminous and heavy textbooks. In the quiet of her room
she must think through and work through the problems
assigned her in class, in order to master them by her own
intellectual efforts and assimilate them in her mind. Books
are there to help her. They are the valuable friends of
her mind. Sometimes she is pleased with the many books
surrounding her, sometimes she reproaches them. She loves
a book that helps her solve a problem, come a step closer
to the truth for which she is searching. She praises such
a book, "You're wonderful; I like you," she sometimes
says. Or she may say to herself, "I really ought to write a
few lines to the author of this good book and thank him
for presenting his problem so clearly."

If she does not understand a subject presented in a book
she is annoyed: "Is this not clear or am I too stupid to
understand it?" she asks herself and reads it again. Then
she closes the book and thinks about it. She knows the
problem must be thought through. "Don't memorize, but
think it through thoroughly and understand it. That is
the important thing." In the quiet of her room she hears
the voice of her professor. She makes a note of the difficulties which block her understanding. She will look up
other books in the library; she will discuss the problem
with her fellow-student who is taking the same course and
who is considered intelligent. In the class discussion she
will tackle the question again. Thus she struggles with the
ideas and problems assigned in lectures and seminars, in
order to build her self-respect, please her parents, impress

the boy who is her friend—in short, in order to have a better life. Each time she enters her room and closes the door behind her she becomes more aware of her striving, for on her desk or on the bookcase she sees photographs of her hard-working father and of her friend. They both think she is intelligent. She must not disappoint them.

If the books in her room tire her she does something else for a change. She writes a letter to the boy who is fond of her and who appreciates her. She talks to her roommate for a while about one thing and another, about the little things that affect their world. She picks out a dress for the next dance and tries it on once again in front of the mirror. She washes her hair, polishes her nails. She may also sit on the terrace of her dormitory and knit for a while or go for a walk along the quiet paths. In winter she builds a snowman in the large campus garden. If she feels like it she will go to the recreation room, smoke a cigarette or drink a cup of coffee, talk to her fellow-students or relax with music. If she has a mind to, she may call up her friend and ask him how life is going in the great world outside.

She may not loaf for long. Knowing that she has not done all her homework, she is driven back to her books, to reading, thinking, understanding. If she again becomes exhausted from studying or if sitting still for so long at her desk has made her uncomfortable, she gets up, changes her clothes and lies down on her bed. She loves her bed upon which her mascot—a charming doll or a little lion—is sitting wide awake. She muses for a while with half-closed eyes. Many fantasies flit through her mind: the grade given her by that brilliant instructor for her excellent report, her name on the dean's list, the new convertible, a present from her father for her achievements, the red roses which her friend will give her on graduation day —in fact, a hundred other images, each more wonderful than the last.[5] Then she awakens again to the real world. She returns to her textbooks and loses herself in her work so that the lovely dream world will one day become reality.

In the morning when the college girl wakes up she finds her calculus or her Russian grammar lying beside her. The first thing she says to her roommate is, "I have two tests today; keep your fingers crossed." If it is a Saturday she will probably say, "I have a date today; I'm looking forward to it."

The classroom is a place where she spends three to six hours a day. It is a plain, clean room. There are a few pictures on the walls. Most of the room is taken up by rows of desk-chairs. Between them and the large blackboard is a desk for the instructor.

When the bell rings for class the college girl enters promptly and confidently, carrying her heavy books and notebooks. If no seat has been assigned to her by the instructor she chooses one she likes. While she is waiting for the teacher, she arranges her books for the lesson or chats quietly with her neighbor. She gets up to greet the entering instructor. The class begins. During the hour she may not remain passive. She is asked questions and encouraged to ask questions of her own. She is sent to the blackboard and she must take notes. She must keep her mind on the subject in order to understand the problem that is presented. If one or another girl forgets herself during the hour and becomes diverted, she is brought back to attention by the alert instructor. She is immediately sorry that she has not been listening. "I beg your pardon," she says courteously and sometimes she blushes.

As a rule there is no difficulty about maintaining classroom order in an American girls' college. The majority of students are industrious, obedient and attentive. They are deeply interested in acquiring the means to probe the mysteries of the universe and of the human spirit. They are not sitting here in the classroom because they must— which is often the case in high school—but because they want to. Basically it was their own wish to come to college and do well in their studies. Thus they accept the rules of order which help them reach their goal more easily. They do so even if they find it hard. For not all of them have previously learned to observe order and to appreciate it. But they are far from perpetrating any foolishness during class, chattering or doing anything that might disturb. They are prevented not only by their good taste but also by their eager determination to cooperate. Moreover, the orderly atmosphere surrounding them on the campus influences them toward adopting a mental concentration which keeps them alertly attentive during class. From this same source they also derive the strength to overcome any tendency toward boredom during the lecture.

As a matter of fact, it is a pleasure for the instructor to teach the American college girl in the classroom or in the laboratory. She works in an agreeable fashion. She is extremely courteous and alert. A glance suffices and the window is closed, the blackboard erased, the book opened. If the instructor corrects her, she thanks him. Her gratitude is not always spoken, but rather implied. It may be read from her expression which borders on the humble, from her embarrassed smile which asks pardon.

She is controlled but informal. In the classroom she feels almost at home. It does not occur to her to be afraid of asking questions, of expressing an opinion about the problem. If she thinks she has something to say she raises her hand, gets up and talks. Quietly, clearly, with simple words she expresses her opinion. If it turns out that she has been mistaken, she is not unhappy about it. She knows that she can also learn by her mistakes. If at times there is a slight embarrassment, it is instantly brushed off with a brief jest. It may come from herself, from the instructor or from a witty fellow-student.

Because she regards the campus as her second home and the classroom as one of many rooms at her disposal, she permits herself certain liberties in it which are perfectly tolerable. Some people may even regard them as agreeably natural, inducing rest and relaxation from concentrated thinking. For example, if she is slightly tired or if she feels cramped, she will not hesitate to change her position or tuck one foot under her on the chair, as though she were sitting beside a country-club fireplace. Sometimes she lays her head on the table for a moment without losing the thread of the lesson. If inadvertently her legs or hands go too far, the instructor or her neighbor quietly calls it to her attention. Then she immediately corrects her posture. One is reminded of an obedient child in a well-bred family. It may also happen that a student will burst out in the middle of a class, "Oh, how pretty, the first snow!" Or, "Look! there's a squirrel knocking at the window. It wants to come in." This scarcely disturbs. Rather, it offers a sudden opportunity to take a deep breath and then turn back refreshed to the matter at hand.

She is cooperative and cheerful. During class she is

friendly and eager to help her teacher and her fellow-students. Entirely on her own, she offers to help the instructor write on the blackboard, pick out books in the library, work with instruments in the laboratory. She offers him her services in copying manuscripts and doing scientific research. When there is an opportunity in class, she also advises her colleagues as to how best solve the problem under discussion. Her cooperation is in no way disturbing. Rather, she helps her companions ascend the path of knowledge more easily. Her sympathy toward her chosen subject, her enthusiasm for the question which still awaits an answer, her wit in asides and her repartee in the question-and-answer duel—these are all characteristics of her alert and lively mind, which make the class lesson an intellectual pleasure for everyone.

In an American girls' college the classroom is the workshop where serious studying and genial cooperation are interspersed with hearty laughter. This would seem to be an ideal field of activity, and by and large it is. But we must add that, just as not all the flowers in a meadow show the same freshness, color and vitality, so not all the girls in class look at one with the same eager and alive faces. We can easily understand why this is so. There is usually something which prevents these girls from applying themselves wholeheartedly to the problem. The chief obstacles are: the subject, a girl's dislike of the classroom, an instructor whom she finds unsympathetic, or a psychological problem during the hour.

She does not like all the subjects she is required to take. But she must enroll for them and master them because they belong to the course of study in her chosen field. With feelings of disinclination and apathy she sits in the classroom in which the subject she does not care for is taught. Her discontent is not obvious; she is too sensible and controlled to show it openly. But one sees it in her facial expression, in the restless way she moves in her seat, in the effort it takes to orient herself to the problem at hand. One can see in her behavior that she is not quite at home in this particular class. Accordingly, she makes a mute demand to be treated like a guest by those who are at home in it. If there is a lack of hospitality, she breathes a sigh of relief at the end of the hour, and leaves the classroom with a "Thank God!" Sometimes one hears her say: "I'll be glad when I'm through with *that* course."

The location and arrangement of the classroom can also cause a feeling of discomfort. Lack of sunlight, a less than desirable view, furnishings which offend her taste, uncomfortable tables or chairs—these can somewhat dampen her enthusiasm from the start. If her interest is aroused and sustained in the course of intensive classwork she usually forgets these incidental annoyances and is able to concentrate once more.

It may also happen that she is not impressed by the instructor. She does not find him compatible; that is to say, she does not like either his teaching method or his personality. She may also find occasion to criticize his approach to the subject or the way in which he treats the class as a whole or herself in particular. Then she presumes to judge him thus: "I like him as a person but not as a teacher; you don't learn much in his course." Or: "He is a good teacher, but it's hard to get along with him. He doesn't show any human interest in his students." But it is not often that one hears: "I can't understand why he became a teacher."

Additional feelings of annoyance can also influence her otherwise attentive and enthusiastic attitude during class. Such moods of depression usually come if she is unprepared, or if she is tired, has slept badly, is overworked or has had bad news.

But the dark clouds of discontent which now and then overshadow her bright enthusiasm for the search for truth in the classroom or the laboratory dissolve in the warm rays of her young, courageous spirit. Filled with love for her studies and for the more attractive life, she conquers her weariness by saying to herself: "The required course which gives you trouble will soon be over. Look forward to the next classroom which is pleasanter than the one you are sitting in. Be nice to the teacher you do not like. Perhaps it is not his fault if he is unable to satisfy all your demands. Try to be doubly attentive if you are unprepared or tired. Later you will have plenty of time to rest and catch up. Don't show that you aren't as good as Gloria, the darling of the class." She rises above aversion and weariness by the self-control and self-encouragement which is practiced on the campus, and uses them to cope with the problem before the class. By means of her self-control in little things, she creates a happy atmosphere of work in the study rooms. Tired or depressed though she is, she nevertheless tries to formulate in proper words the right answer to the question asked. Her fervent effort is wreathed in a faint smile, the dignified smile which animates the intellectual atmosphere of all the rooms of the campus.

If one carefully observes the college girl from the first day of her study to the solemn hour of commencement, one discovers a whole range of emotional response. She arrives fresh, buoyant, filled with energy and the desire to work. This increased feeling of ambition and vitality takes her through her freshman year. There is a waning of this enthusiasm in the sophomore year, but her spirit still shows traces of her first outburst of love for campus life. Usually, in her junior year, she goes through a crisis. We then find but little of the student's initial enthusiasm for her studies and for the campus world. She often looks tired, listless, almost indifferent. A mood of lethargy and discomfort has taken hold of her. She no longer looks like someone pleased to be a college girl, but more like one who feels the title to be an imposition. In her final year, as a senior, she shows still another side in her behavior. She presents a picture of longing directed toward a goal which will soon be fulfilled: she will presently be liberated from the daily routine of campus life, and set free to realize her plans and ideals out in the world. This consciousness gives her the strength to make her final months and days a pattern of excellence.

One can well understand the reasons for such changes of mood. As a freshman and sophomore she cherishes the wish to prove herself as a college girl, to be more than an average student. Besides, everything is new to her at first. The novelty stirs her interest, keeps her fresh, stimulates her to become familiar with the unfamiliar. By the time she has become a junior, she is familiar with all the situations of campus life. She need no longer show that she is capable of mastering higher education. She has also grown accustomed to the glamor of the name "college girl." It no longer impresses her. Campus life has become routine, and often vexes her with petty annoyances. The thought of having to struggle two more years with books, instructors and academic problems also contributes to her weariness with the campus atmosphere which, theoretically, continues to remain attractive. It is astonishing how even loveliness, when continuous, can sometimes bore us.

When she reaches the senior year she feels like a person preparing for a journey into the great world. There is no time left to be melancholy, annoyed or indifferent. So many things remain to be done before she is quite ready to step onto the stage in that theater of life beyond the campus. The shorter the time, the more she realizes that there were many good things on the campus of which she was not aware. A feeling of sadness comes over her when she thinks of them. It is this sort of contemplation which impels her to constructive effort and gives her dignity and maturity. The fluctuations of feeling which the college girl is bound to experience during her student days on the campus are particularly noticeable to the person who is in close contact with her. Her moods of sympathy and antipathy are especially pronounced in class. Here the sharp eye of the instructor sees not only that she is there, but how she is there. The way she speaks and writes, the way she thinks and looks, the way she sits and gets up— all this reflects her inner struggle with the situation and with life in general. Helping her in this struggle, which means shaping her intellect, is a noble service. It proves to be a joy both for those who serve and those who are served. Thus the relationship between students and teachers in the classroom has radiations of mutual joy which stream beyond campus boundaries.

The library is another study room in which the college girl spends much time. It is an important retreat for her. Here her mind and soul are nourished. Here she reads and writes, studies and does research. Many rooms are at her disposal, equipped with desks and comfortable chairs. There are even studio couches in the corners where she can make herself comfortable if she chooses. Portraits and statues of learned men and women look down upon her and invite her, wordlessly, to slake her thirst for knowledge at the springs they have tapped. Here are many attendants who, in a friendly spirit, offer her access to the books that deal with the knowledge she is seeking and the wisdom to which she aspires. She finds books large and small, thick and thin, heavy and light, wherever she looks. Here, they are patiently waiting for her attention, a huge selection for her needs. She cannot consult all of them; she cannot read many of them. She devotes herself only to some, and only a few win her heart. But she cannot get along without them. Constantly concerned with the cultivation of her inner world, she knows that her mind needs books as urgently as her body needs bread and water. That is why she loves the many books in the library, just as she relishes the many kinds of food in the cafeteria.

The college girl has a great deal to do in the library. We see her burying herself in a book recommended by one of the instructors, making notes, meditating with closed eyes about important ideas in order to understand them thoroughly and fix them in her memory. We observe her carefully leafing through old books and manuscripts, searching for material for her assigned report. Here she must often consult the dictionaries and encyclopedias. They help explain words and concepts. She needs to be clear about words and concepts so that she can accurately and successfully master the problems posed in school and in life. If her hands grow tired from handling heavy reference books and her eyes fatigued from fine print, she takes up a lighter book with larger print. This is dessert for her mind.

The following conversation between two students was overheard in a college library by the author:

"Enough reading for today! Let's go to the cafeteria and get something to eat," the first girl proposed.

"Do you know," said the other, "when I read Saint Exupéry I forget that I'm hungry or thirsty. On every page he offers something that makes me happy."

"It's the same way with me when I read Kafka," said her companion.

At times she takes a brief stroll through the library. She walks around and looks at the books. Often she discovers one that piques her curiosity. Carefully she picks it up and makes its acquaintance. She pays a brief visit to the books in the exhibition room. They are displayed for her, they are waiting to be noticed by her. Then she spends a little time in the new book section to see what has recently appeared and to have one or another book reserved if it interests her. In the periodical room she looks through the latest issues of journals dealing with her subject. She also glances at others that take her fancy. If she finds something that interests her she sits right down and reads. If, on her intellectual stroll, she sees a friend or classmate who is not too deeply engrossed in her books, she sits down beside her for a brief whispered chat for relaxation. Then when she gets up and moves on, books again meet her glance. In all the rooms, along all the walls and in all the corners they look down on the college girl. Often it seems to her that her world consists of books and nothing else.

She appreciates great books that are there to nourish her mind and nurture her soul. She knows that Dante found consolation for the death of Beatrice in Cicero's *De Amicitia* and Boethius' *De Consolatione Philosophiae*.

Another place where the college girl spends a couple of hours every day is the dining hall. Here she has breakfast, lunch and dinner. Mainly she must serve herself. The large dining hall resembles many others which, equipped for self-service, are to be found in clubs and various community institutions throughout the United States. Simple, comfortable chairs and tables, a few choice pictures on the walls, tasteful curtains at the windows— these are all things which are to be found in other dining rooms. The unique thing in the dining room on the campus is the college girl herself and her behavior. She handles dishes and silver carefully and quietly. She sits up straight and eats in a deliberate, seemly manner. She does not look merely at her own plate, nor think only of herself. She is concerned not only with her own food and enjoyment. She is also thoughtfully attentive of her tablemates and helps them. She voluntarily serves those sitting on either side of her by offering them the salt or the sugar or whatever else they may need and does so quietly and courteously. If she overlooks some small service, she excuses herself gently: "Pardon me, I should have noticed that." If she does not like the food she will hardly say, "It doesn't taste good, I don't like it." Rather, "My mother cooks it differently!" Or: "At home things do taste better." Or she is silent and thinks: perhaps I am not hungry. Once in a Latin class we translated the sentence: "Hunger is the best sauce." If a dish tastes particularly good to her she will say, beaming, "It is excellent!" Now and then she adds something amusing, such as, "That's the way I'm going to cook some day for my children and my husband." She has to laugh as she says it, an almost imperceptible blush spreads over her still childlike face.

Her table conversation is not always very witty, but it is amusing and meant to be relaxing. She likes to laugh and she laughs often. Usually she tells about little things that happen in her everyday world.

Her elegant little head is abundantly tortured in the classroom and the library, and, even in the dining hall scientific problems and ideas keep running through it, but it enjoys a complete change in the gymnasium and on the sports field. Here she plays handball, table tennis and other games. Here she runs fast, falls, picks herself up and runs again. Here she shouts, laughs aloud and whistles. Here she dances.

The way she plays commands attention. We are not referring primarily to her technique, but rather to her ethical and esthetic behavior on the field. Her movements in the game are not always perfect—after all, she does not play as a professional—but the way she handles herself is always impressive. Her feeling for rules, her cooperation with her teammates, her respect and tolerance toward her opponents are always admirable. The fact that she throws herself into the game, offends no one, has a kind, encouraging word for her fellow-student in the midst of the game, sends her opponent a friendly smile, and can laugh heartily even if she doesn't make it, if she loses the game— is not all this a joyful discovery for the spectator who is looking for spiritual standards?

In spring, she plays outdoors on the campus athletic

field. Clothed in a light, short sports dress she plays tennis, golf or hockey. Gentle sunshine, dust-free air, green trees and colorful flowers all around make a charming setting for her play and she, the player, blends inimitably with this radiance. One need not be a poet in order to see something wonderful in this harmony.

Once on a sunny spring day, I took a stroll across the campus with a philosophy instructor. At the edge of the sports field, a pretty student was sitting on a rock, her hair slightly disheveled, her face a fresh rosy color, her legs dangling. She was inhaling deeply the spring aroma of blossoming trees. As she rested, leaning against her hockey stick, her bright eyes were following the ball as it flew back and forth between the sticks of her teammates. "A magnificent creature in this magnificent setting," remarked my colleague, adding, "If Schopenhauer could have seen this picture, his pessimism about the world and human beings would probably have taken on a brighter hue." In spring and autumn, on days when the sun is warm and gentle, she finds an opportunity to stretch out in her bathing suit in some remote corner of the campus, in order to brown in the sun, to forget the daily grind for a while in the company of sun, wind and fragrant flowers, to experience consciously and enjoy with all her senses the beauty and goodness of nature. Here birds, small rabbits and squirrels entertain her. These are the domestic animals of the campus, tamed, protected and loved. They dance a dance of sympathy and trust around the girl. She has made pets of the little animals; she may enjoy their pleasant company.

"It is wonderful to lie here, arms and legs stretched out, not to think about anything or do anything," she says to the girl lying near her. But after a while: "Did you bring your calculus with you? I'm having trouble with a problem in it." A squirrel comes running toward her and politely asks for a nut. She throws him one. "That solves your problem. Ah, to be carefree, it's so wonderful."

Another place on the campus that pleases and refreshes her during her free time is the swimming pool. Here she plays with the water. She slips into it not only to be cleansed and refreshed—that she takes for granted—but with the thought of how to invent new forms and finer techniques in swimming strokes and dives, and how to execute them gracefully. She is concerned about the movement of her body in the water. Playfully she struggles with ever new and ever finer forms and lines which turn into a dance with the blue transparent water.

Submerged to her lips, she stays in the water a long time. She lets herself be permeated to the uttermost nerve and the innermost vein of her body, by the freshness, the warmth or the coolness of the water. This gives her a feeling of well-being which she loves. It is the feeling of mysterious warmth or coolness sensed through the medium of wetness. She gives voice to this intensified perception, "It's wonderful," and one realizes the truth of her words in her beaming face, in the graceful movements of her buoyant body. Now and then one also hears her say: "I feel reborn."

Sometimes when she is playing with the water she thinks of her friend.[6] If, in swimming, she succeeds in drawing a flexible and unusual line with the sweep of her body, she says to herself, "If only he could see this!" But if she has difficulty in executing a new attractive nuance in her water dance, she thinks, "If only he were here! He would help me, hold me up, let me go and then take my hand, again and again, until I succeed. Then he would take me in his arms, and would carry me—and tired and exhausted, I would feel as if I were floating."

Another pleasant way of spending her free time is walking. In the United States walking—except for so-called window shopping in cities—has been almost abandoned. Instead of walking, people go driving. On the campus, the college girl seldom has a car, so she goes on foot. But she does this even if her parents have given her the use of a car. She is lured out of doors by blossoms in springtime, white snow in winter, colorful leaves in autumn, by shaded avenues and well-tended paths. She cannot resist this beauty. On her walks she admires the flowers. She pauses for a time beside a flower, her favorite. It may be a rose or a lily or some other species that moves her. Bent over, as if in devotion, she touches the flower gently and breathes deeply its indescribable fragrance. "You will have a place in the garden I shall some day have," she says softly. If she meets hungry squirrels, she tosses them nuts that she has remembered to take along. If a saucy little rabbit crosses her path she chases it for a minute; her heart begins to beat faster and that feels good. It gives the breeze blowing from the wide fragrant meadows or the blue lake freer access to her lungs and her heart.

In winter she builds snowmen in the large campus garden. This is great fun. Dressed in high boots and a thick pullover, she rolls the snow and makes a figure—a snowman or a Santa Claus. The lower part is easy, but the upper part, the face of the snowman, gives her trouble. Sometimes it's too big, sometimes too small, sometimes too oval or not funny enough. She labors to achieve an original form, an image she has somewhere in her critical mind's eye, as she shakes the soft white snow. For her the snowman she has created is alive. "Listen, the wind is playing a tune for us, my dear snowman, come and dance with me on the soft white earth," she says to her handiwork, embracing it and laughing heartily. Her companions laugh with her. Enviable laughter over sublime nothings!

Sometimes she walks up and down the quiet avenues of the campus. She goes alone or with an intimate friend. They talk little. This is the time for meditation, for quiet observation, for inner listening. Indeed, it is the quiet that she finds comforting. Sometimes it is as important for her spirit as water is for her thirsty body. She needs silence in order to be alone with herself. Looking out over the distant fields or woods, the mountains or the sea, she remembers the living and the dead who are close to her. At such times she meets the members of her family and her friends; but the image of an artist or scientist whom she has perhaps never seen also rises up before her admiring soul. Or she is reminded of the unsolved problem, the unanswered letter, an unpressed dress for the next evening dance. During this quiet walk, important and unimportant matters well up from her subconscious and beg to be straightened out. Such a walk is in the nature of a dialogue with herself, her conscience. It is a quiet stroll in the soothing atmosphere of natural beauty which is conducive to meditation, which wordlessly summons her to enter a higher stage of reality and of order.

If she has time, she leaves the confines of the campus in order to see how things are going in the world outside. She moves in crowded streets, among speeding cars, noisy children, hurrying people with careworn faces. If she compares this world with her own on the campus she concludes: how different are these two worlds! And her ears pick up the words she heard during her first days on the campus: You have come into this small, beautiful world so that, later on, you will be able to make an honorable mark in the larger world. Faced by these two different worlds, she is moved by strange, probably idealistic thoughts: I shall influence the city council to keep the streets cleaner; I shall drive slower and more carefully; I shall not permit my children to make so much noise; I shall try to keep my husband's mind free of worry.

She enters a small, cozy coffee shop. Here she refreshes herself by ordering a cup of coffee, a glass of Coca Cola, or a dish of ice cream. If she has taken up smoking, she lights a cigarette with poise and deliberation. With a friend or with acquaintances from the campus she talks about the personalities and events of her world, just as they occur to her. It is relaxing for her to be away from classrooms, not to see books and teachers for a while, to talk and laugh in other surroundings. She is filled with a gentle feeling of well-being as she observes life on the street from the windows of the coffee shop. She sees pictures of the everyday life of the great world. It is like a stage on which scenes appear and disappear. Some of these scenes remind her of childhood experiences and lead her imagination into the world of dreams. But this can not go on for long. A girl who has just glanced at her watch cries, "Time to go home." They go home—to the campus.

When she returns, a little fatigued from a long walk, the college girl finds a comfortable home waiting for her.

the steps of her dormitory she turns around once more, as though she wanted to bid a friendly farewell and say "Thank you" to all the clean paths and quiet avenues, all the kind flowers and green trees, to the warming sun and soothing clouds, as though she wanted to say, "All of you have given me pleasure!"

On the campus there is one other place which is meant neither for work nor for play, but for prayer. It is the campus chapel. Here she attends community services, but she comes alone, too, in order to be silent and undisturbed with God. She stands before Him with her intimate sorrows and joys, in humility and simplicity. This is the place where she can see herself utterly naked, for there can be no pretence or deception before God. You stand before Him as you really are. This realization, based on meditation and conscience-searching, cleanses and elevates her soul.

Her meditation finds release in prayer and thanksgiving. She prays to the Father of heaven and earth that He shall be with her always and protect her soul from all ills, that He shall help her live and die in His love. Here she thanks God for the good parents He gave her, for the health she enjoys, for her happy life on the campus, for her good grade in the last test, even for the fun she had at the last dance. In this spirit of thanksgiving and humble prayer she reverently lingers in the chapel where the consciousness of indestructible beauty illumines her soul. The light of this beauty shines in her eyes. With her face transfigured by this mood of exaltation, she steps out of chapel in order to take up her daily life and master it in the spirit of beauty.

No matter where the college girl goes on the campus,

she is everywhere directly or indirectly challenged to work on herself, on the beauty of her spirit and the cultivation of her body. Everything she hears, sees and reads moves her to higher forms of self-education to which she joyfully devotes herself. Her life is like a symphony which contains nothing tragic or dramatic, but which unfolds gaily and lightly in a thousand little pleasures. It is a human life embodying the music of the young Mozart.

Her Appearance

Her entire appearance, though carefully, almost scrupulously planned and worked out, has the effect of being an unplanned design.

In the preceding chapters we have become acquainted with the environment in which the American college girl lives, studies and plays. We have had a glimpse of a world planned and shaped for the cultivation of her soul and body, and, fleetingly, of the college girl herself living, studying and playing in this world. Now let us step closer and become more thoroughly acquainted with the college girl. First of all we shall concern ourselves with her external appearance. In this chapter we intend to show how she dresses and how she is groomed, how she speaks and laughs, how she sits, stands and walks.

She makes an art of clothing herself. It gives her a great deal of pleasure to play with the many colors and variations of fashion. She would scarcely maintain that clothes make the woman. Women make clothes, she says to herself, without giving it much thought, and she chooses her clothes to suit her own taste. In selecting her wardrobe she has a number of advisers: her mother, her older sister or a friend, fashion magazines, the experienced personnel in the college shop of a large department store. Sometimes her boy friend also gives her a few hints, usually indirectly, about what he would like to see her wear. But hers is the final decision. Pattern and style must please her taste. How does her taste show itself in her clothes?

The college girl dresses simply. We do not find anything extravagant, ostentatious or extreme in her clothes. Neither style nor colors are showy. If she had an ambition in high school to make an impression with her clothes, to attract attention, she has given it up in college, for the sake of the simplicity which she now regards as a classic virtue. It makes her laugh to think how enthusiastic she used to be about loud colors and an exciting style, how she tried to outdo her classmates in the matter of dress. Now she is proud of her more refined taste which she has acquired in the college atmosphere and which she can express every day in new and different ways. The college girl is agreeably outstanding by the very unobtrusiveness of her clothes.

She is less conspicuously dressed than many other girls who are not in college. By inconspicuous we do not mean mousy; we associate it with the simple design, the harmonious, subtle colors of conservative taste. Gray, somewhat on the dark side, and a soft white is a combination which gives her appearance a charming and refined touch.

She is scrupulously clean when it comes to her clothes. She does not tolerate a speck of dust or a single spot. A tiny spot on her skirt makes her uncomfortable until she has managed to remove it with soap and water. She is also anxious to have her clothes in order. Not a button may be missing. A rip would cause her embarrassment. However, she is never excessively self-conscious. Sometimes, though rarely, her petticoat shows or the ends of the shoulder straps of her bra can be seen under her blouse. But because her underclothing is always fresh and clean, this is not disturbing, in fact, it adds something essential, it completes the picture of her grooming. It shows how natural her way of dressing is.

She looks as though she felt free and comfortable in her clothes. Nothing that she wears impedes her movements. On the contrary, her light, casual clothing carries her along the various paths marked out by her daily routine. In her clothes she feels like a bird in its feathers. There is nothing she avoids more than clothes that may look artificial on her or make her feel stiff. Her gift for the purely natural in her appearance is amazing. One has the impression that she would rather look a bit untidy than artificial or stiff. Even the skirt and pullover which are designed to outline the natural contours of her body must not be so tight or provocative that they restrict her freedom of movement or distort her charm.

The college girl dresses with originality. Or rather, she makes clothes look original on herself. She gets ideas from fashion magazines, fashion shows, clothes that she sees in window displays or that she observes on other girls who are tastefully dressed. But the moment she puts on an article of clothing that she has bought it looks as though it had been designed and made just for her. Why is that? She adapts it to suit her taste by changing something, adding something or taking something away so that it will conform to her figure or to the color of her hair and

eyes. But this is not the most essential part of her originality. Here, as in everything, her mental attitude is decisive; it permeates her self and everything she wears.
The logical relationship between her young, gracefully
controlled body and the clothes she chooses produces a
rare picture. Individual blending of colors, individual
ways of doing her hair, individuality in her choice of
unobtrusive jewelry gives this picture a vivid sense of
personality. In the subtle relationship of mind, body and
matter the college girl's appearance proves to be individual and unique.

Clothes and jewelry help her to overcome the everyday
monotony. They give her a chance to reveal ever new
pictures and forms of esthetic enjoyment. A different
frock, a different skirt, a different blouse, different shoes,
a different way of doing her hair, everything that is becoming and pleasing changes her appearance. In this way
she always gives herself and her environment something
new. This pleases her and everyone who is privileged to
see her. Her pleasure in her "new" look created by color
and line is devoid of any egotism. For her the frequent
change of clothing is nothing more than a conscious search
for possibilities of expressing within her own person
nuances of beauty for herself and for others.

She wears different clothes during the day, when she
attends lectures, in the evening when she appears at dinner, when she attends a club meeting or goes out, when
she dresses for a birthday party. On weekdays in class,
in the library or at meals in the cafeteria, one finds her
dressed in blouse and skirt, wearing comfortable shoes
which resemble house slippers rather than street shoes.
Her boyish hair combed fairly straight does not worry

her. Thus, decently and cleanly dressed she looks like the daughter of a self-respecting family. The same girl looks entirely different when you see her, now and then, on the dance floor. Here she wears high-heeled shoes, an elegant full-skirted dress, her lightly perfumed hair shines in the soft indirect light from the bar, which is also reflected in the wine glasses. Her movements remind one of those of a young dancer who appreciates herself in her art. Does she realize, this dancing college girl, that the person looking at her, one who does not even know her name, also takes pleasure in her existence, her appearance?

Like every other woman in the world, the American woman wants to stay young and pretty. The country's highly developed cosmetics industry offers her plenty of opportunity for this. But it is interesting to observe that, although girls in the public schools of the country apply lipstick and rouge freely, the college girl makes little use of them. In class she usually appears without make-up. Sometimes she uses lip rouge, lightly, dexterously, usually in a shade approximating the natural color of her lips. It is only on special occasions that she gives more attention to her face. But even then she uses cosmetics with great care and precision, merely to accent her features delicately. In order to improve her appearance she shapes her lips, and carefully works on her eyebrows and lashes. For her a well applied make-up is a minor creative activity which she performs not out of vanity but for the sake of beauty.

Well-groomed hands belong to a well cared-for face. She knows that not everyone can have beautiful hands, but every girl can have beautifully cared-for hands. The first thing one looks at is the face; then one's glance usually falls on the hands. She herself always sees her hands. She must be satisfied with them, and they must please others. Therefore she devotes time and care to their grooming. She realizes how attractive it is to touch beautiful things, to stroke something lovely, to offer something graciously with beautifully cared-for hands.

At the sight of these tenderly cared-for hands one would instinctively like to press them gently when they are outstretched in greeting, to hold them chastely in dancing, to be served by these lovely and gracious hands. But this does not mean that one desires them or falls in love with them. It resembles the wish one sometimes has to touch the petals of a rose.

"Smile" is an inscription that is often seen in America in offices, hotels, factories and other public places. From the very first days of life, a child is taught to smile. Photographers refuse to take a picture of a face, especially that of a woman, without a smile. Hence the pictures in American newspapers are almost always smiling. A country of smiles? Yes, on the campus—always.[7]

This smile consciously taught and sometimes propagated throughout a lifetime is not always spontaneous. It may be unnatural and affected and lack depth and warmth because people smile too often for no reason, not from inner necessity, but simply from habit, impelled by the motto: "Smile!" This is not true of the college girl's smile. She does not fix her lips into a smile as though a mask had been placed on them. Her smile breaks out spontaneously; it is fresh and warm, reflected in her eyes. It is a smile that in its genuineness can be compared with that of a child. Whether it is an expression of gaiety, well-being or friendliness, it is always an unadulterated outpouring of her heart.

But her smile or her laughter has a characteristic note

which can be described as discipline or control. That is to say, her laughter is restrained, decent, mastered. This does not mean that it is "frozen" or artificial. On the contrary, it is distilled, purified, refined, and it has greater charm for two reasons. First, it reveals control of the mind, by which the higher levels of tact are governed; secondly, we feel that it is laughter coming from the fullness of the heart. We realize that not all of the girl's happiness or sympathy is poured forth by her lips. Rather, they give out only a small ray of that warm radiance which dwells in her heart.

Hidden in her laughter there is a certain shrewdness which sometimes borders on irony. A cultured attaché of a large Western power once lectured at a college foreign language club. Nearly every third word had a wrong accent. The college girl smiled. Another time a spontaneous and emotional speaker lectured on the aims of American youth. He constantly and pathetically reiterated the phrase, "It's wonderful to be alive!" The college girl smiled. A young Latin instructor told me how he once used a pony to translate a text, and was caught at it by a student. "Did she say anything?" I asked. "She said nothing, she merely smiled," he replied.

But the college girl can also laugh at herself. A professor once pointed out to a student a sentence in her work which had no principal clause. She laughed. "What do you find so amusing about that?" the professor, who had a touch of the European tradition about him, asked, somewhat annoyed. "I am laughing at my own stupidity, Professor!" the college girl replied.

A friend of mine, an educator and psychologist, with whom I discussed the college girl said that one should also consider her voice. It is a clear, agreeable, soothing voice in which one cannot as yet detect any disappointment, depression or nervousness, and seldom a slight weariness. In the inflection of her voice, the articulation of her words, the expressions of her face there is a mixture of naiveté and sobriety. The naïve element in the inflection betrays the childlike quality of her spirit; the sobriety in the manner of her expression shows her well-developed reasoning power, her understanding of the situation. It is the voice of a child who is already able to think. More than that. The naive or childlike quality which becomes manifest in her way of speaking and her ability to express herself clearly combine into an organic unity to such an extent that her voice sounds joyous, almost gay. The modulation of her voice, the inflection, the timbre, her whole manner of speaking is the product of standards which are rooted in her entire upbringing, and are nurtured by the college atmosphere. These standards, it should be noted, have been acquired indirectly rather than directly. They have gradually acquired the force of habit, have been assimilated into her whole personality, and are finally as certain as instinct. Therefore it seems as though the college girl had been born with the art of elegant speech.

Naturally, girls also come to college who are not sufficiently at home in this cultivated manner of speaking. But on the campus they soon learn to master it. A first year student was asked by her professor to speak a little louder, whereupon she said: "My roommate who is a senior said that a college girl should not raise her voice, that it is not well-bred." When the college girl is talking with friends, with her instructors, or with strangers, whether privately at the tea table, or publicly on the platform, her voice is always clear, controlled, bright. You hear a communicative voice, without timidity or haughteur, without exaggerated emotion and without soporific monotony. In the timbre of her voice one hears a cordial friendliness which wells up from her idealistic spirit and seeks to reach the soul of the listener. It is a voice which gives more than it demands.

You discover the quality of her speech especially in personal conversation with her. It is not what she says, but how she says it that counts. One must be aware not only of the sound but of her whole manner of expression in order to discover its magic. When one hears her speak and at the same time sees her eyes, her lips, her entire countenance, one has a picture with which one would like to linger. What is it that attracts? It is the radiation of her spirit which gives warmth to her speech.

All the characteristics which have been mentioned are brought into harmonious unity by the charm of her movements. The melody of her movement animates her clothes, her make-up, her hands, her smile and her voice. The college girl's movements have the character of gay elegance. It is a well-bred movement with playful intervals. Her elegance and breeding can be traced back to the careful cultivation of her subjective world. Her gaiety or playfulness arises from the spontaneity of youth which is not yet burdened with great cares. Her step is light and supple, like that of a person whose body has not yet become a burden. She can run like a boy. But she can also step out like a young dancer, nimble and fascinating. Her sparse gestures which occasionally emphasize a thought, the alert look of her searching eyes, the relaxed and yet flexible way she turns around—all this is sustained by a gay elegance suffused with grace and charm. Her movement is like a well thought out and well-expressed composition which, however, is perfectly natural in its expression. Often her movement abandons the sphere of refinement and becomes humorous. This saves her from appearing stiff and dull. Whether she walks, stands or sits, her bearing is always adapted to the situation. She masters each movement with deft sureness and simple grace. Even when a feeling of disappointment or exasperation grips her, she struggles valiantly against it and consciously suppresses it because it spoils her charm.

We discover the secrets of what is called an aristocratic bearing if we observe how she studies the questions on an examination sheet, how she looks at the first snowfall, how she laughs in company, or gives a stranger directions; if we look at her hands as they open a new book in the library, or raise a cocktail glass to her lips; if now and then we see how gracefully she folds her legs as she half reclines on the sofa, or how she moves them as she dances. And if you watch her addressing an audience you may perceive her "mental and spiritual sensibility" in handling the task, "exquisite delicacy" in her movements, her controlled speech.

When you see a college girl fence, her pose reminds you of the graceful form of Penthesilea, the warrior queen, who "with a pointed dart in her maiden hand, with a golden belt fastened beneath her thrust-out breasts, dares to oppose the manly force,"[8] as well as on that of Camilla, the girl athlete, who was "able to outstrip the winds with the swiftness of her feet."[9]

The charm of her movements may be compared to that of a fountain ever changing, yet ever the same. The separate motions may be likened to the drops that, as the sun illuminates them, shine like jewels.

The following letter which a young businessman wrote to his parents about his sister illustrates the appearance of the American college girl and the impression she makes:

"Last Saturday I again visited Sandra on the campus. You know how much I like to be there. It is a real treat for me to get out of the tumult of the big city and forget it for a while among the lovely trees and flowers and the well-tended grounds.

"We talked on the terrace of her dormitory. Sandra had on a dress which, she said, she had taken in at the waist because it was too big for her. It was a very simple dress, white with wide blue stripes, but it was very becoming to her. In fact, I had no fault to find, everything was perfect: her hair, her face, her hands. She told me a lot about her campus life and smiled as she spoke. It was a sympathetic, outgoing smile, accompanied by a soft voice. Her whole bearing was quiet and serene. I felt like saying to her: 'I didn't know I had such a cultivated and impressive sister.' Frankly, dear parents, I never noticed these subtleties so much in her at home. In the dining hall where we had a cup of coffee together Sandra introduced me to a few of her fellow-students. They were all very nice, polite girls. Sandra called one of them her 'big sister.' This is the one she wrote you about who helps her with her calculus. You can tell that she is really a very intelligent girl just by the look in her eyes. I told her that I had heard a lot about her mathematical talents. She didn't want to hear this at all and blushed slightly. She said that they help each other and that Sandra shows everyone how to play a good game of tennis.

"I must also tell you about a music student who entertained us very charmingly by relating an incident in the life of Beethoven. It was really relaxing for me.

"Everything there has a restful effect: objects, flowers, and girls' faces. It is a small, cultivated world where you see and experience only gay and lovely things. But at this point a thoughtful person might instinctively ask: 'How will these girls find their way about when one day they leave this sheltered world and are obliged to assert themselves in the big world which, after all, holds so many disappointments, failures and difficulties?' But then, if you look at them you discover a confidence in their eyes, which is reassuring. Besides, I think they all often dream about a strong prince who will one day protect them from all dangers.

"Sandra accompanied me to the edge of the campus. She asked me when I had been home last and how you were and whether our little Rolf liked kindergarten. I promised to take her out to dinner next Sunday. It can only make one proud to be seen in public with her."

A person might counter all this by saying: "You don't necessarily have to be a college girl in order to be charming and elegant." It is true, there are many girls who have never attended college and who nevertheless show good taste in their clothes and their make-up. They also have pleasant voices and attractive smiles; their hands are well-groomed and their movements have a natural charm. They have a refined bearing, it will be said. This may be true. But there are degrees of refinement. There are roses which are beautiful but have no fragrance; but there are others which are beautiful and have a lovely fragrance. There are diamonds which sparkle brilliantly; and there are some that sparkle more brilliantly because they are more beautifully cut.

The art of her make-up, whether fixed for casual or formal occasions, is an art that conceals art; it is never conspicuous. Her entire appearance, though carefully, almost scrupulously planned and worked out, has the effect of being an unplanned design. And this is precisely what strikes one as elegance and charm. It strikes one simply for not attempting to be striking.

What makes the college girl different from the rest of her contemporaries is her spiritual attitude. That is to say, each external expression of her whole being is illuminated by intellectual radiations. They reflect the cultivated spirit of the girl. In other words, they are evidence of the larger treasures and beauty of her inner world. We must, however, emphasize the fact that it would be erroneous to assume that a girl in other surroundings and by other means could attain the higher stages of refined conduct proper to the college girl without the college atmosphere, without having lived on the campus. If one tried to prove this by pointing to examples, I am afraid one would come to the conclusion that the image sought for and achieved is mainly a substitute for the genuine image presented by the college girl. It should be noted that the external appearance of the college girl, as it has been described in these pages, is not so much the result of formal training in the lecture halls as a product of the entire college and campus atmosphere which can scarcely be found elsewhere and in which the very soul of the girl is organically unfolded.

Her appearance reflects her inner world, the formation of which requires discipline and even a measure of suffering. She is, however, conscious of the wisdom contained in the saying: "It is necessary to suffer in order to be beautiful." For this purpose she commits herself to the hardships imposed upon her by the intellectual and aesthetic pursuits, the sources of real beauty.

Her Subjective World

She is stimulated to think.

Now that we have become acquainted with the college girl's environment and have an idea of her appearance, we shall try to reveal her subjective world. First we shall explore the sources which feed her soul and her spirit. Then we shall give a few illustrations, on the basis of which we may deduce the manifold features of her inner life. But before that we should like to say a few words about the importance of proper nourishment in education.

Experienced gardeners tell us that the quality of flowers and vegetables depends largely on the soil in which they grow. The better the ground is prepared, the better it is; flowers become more beautiful, vegetable plants larger. Even the fragrance of flowers and the flavor of vegetables are affected by the quality of the soil. The excellence of the plant is thus determined by the nature of the soil which nourishes it.

The same is true of animals. The gloss and strength of a horse, for example, are essentially the result of the food it gets. In every piece of meat one can taste the food that the animal was fed. Sometimes pork tastes of the kitchen scraps the animal was fed. The appearance of an animal and the taste of its meat bear the stamp of its nourishment.

The well-being of the human body is likewise dependent on the quality of food and its preparation, a factor which also strongly influences the spiritual and mental state of the human being. I once heard someone say, "We complain nowadays about the disobedience and unruliness of youth. What can we expect if children are no longer reared on mother's milk but on cow's milk or formulas?"

It is well known and need not be pointed out that the college girl, both on and off the campus, is well taken care of. Besides, good bodily nourishment is not among the principal factors that make her a college girl. It is more important to trace the sources and components of the nourishment available to her mind.

There is an old proverb which says: "If you have two loaves of bread, sell one and with the proceeds buy chrysanthemums—food for your soul."

Education in a college offering superior intellectual nourishment is a matter of much effort and expense. Many girls earn their way during vacation, some even during the school year. This is strenuous. Nor is it easy always to be fresh and ready to accept the spiritual nourishment offered, the better to digest it. But the college girl gladly assumes the burden, for she reaps her reward from day to day: her knowledge and her thinking are enriched, her soul expands. Even good physical nourishment must be earned with effort. But it is worthwhile. You remain healthy and full of enterprise and this gives you strength to be active in matters of the spirit.

The college girl is well aware of the fact that she is made up of body and soul, and she also realizes that the spiritual is more valuable than the physical which ages and disintegrates. Throughout her study she makes sacrifices for the sake of her spiritual fare, convinced that in a well-nourished and carefully cultivated spirit, human life becomes easier and more beautiful.

As a rule the college girl is obliged to take about sixteen to twenty hours a week of class work in her major as well as in her electives. In most colleges the following subjects are required: logic, elements of psychology, religion, philosophy of education, history of Western civilization, history of art, history of natural sciences.

She is stimulated to think. Her methods of thinking are guided by standards and laws which give clarity and insight to her intellectual world. Many theories of the structure and functions of the human spirit are expounded to her so that she will know and understand herself and others better.

Man's immortality is revealed to her in many different interpretations. As she struggles for truths which form a bridge to immortality, the feeling that in her, too, not everything is mortal becomes consolidated in a consciousness which gives support to her life.

She is introduced to the problems of education. Old and new methods, classic and modern aims of education are presented to her. The centuries-long struggle for the perfection of human capabilities is discussed. The difference between character training and intellectual training is made clear to her. The relationship between education and self-discipline is pointed out.

The rise and fall of Western cultural history, as well as

of world history is offered to her in fascinating ways. With amazement she sees the tragic panorama of human history. The death of Socrates, of Cicero, the persecution of Galileo, the execution of Marie Antoinette, the murder of innocent Jews at Auschwitz fill her with puzzled horror. Her expression clearly says, "How can a human being be a wolf to his fellow man?" Agitation of this kind enlarges her sympathies and opens up new perspectives for contemplating and understanding man's fate in the universe. This makes her more serious and more mature.[10]

In lectures and seminars she is also introduced to the world of art. By means of abstract and concrete examples she is initiated into the secrets of beauty. Here her aesthetic consciousness is awakened; in other words, she is taught good taste in that type of music and art which is subject to no fashion. Art activity gives her a never-ending pleasure, and in its depths all sorrow is buried.

Another field which arouses her intense interest, is natural science. Here she encounters secrets of the universe that have been uncovered and that can be used for the welfare of humanity as well as for its destruction. She is also introduced to the as yet undiscovered mysteries. She is overwhelmed by the omnipotent genius of the creator of these mysteries and is led toward humility. But the diligence of the servants who are probing these mysteries stimulates her and spurs her on toward cooperation. Often, as she stands on the edge, she is dimly aware of the implication that the least revelation of a secret in science and art means an honor for its creator, rapture for its discoverer and joy for all.

The college girl spends most of her time on her major subject. Whether it is Latin, chemistry or music, it becomes the field of interest that stays closest to her heart, an undertaking of her own choice. She studies and investigates it with patience, inclination and curiosity. If in other subjects her striving is at times relaxed or she seems a bit careless and her industry leaves something to be desired, in her own field she is always alert and zealous, bent on progress. In the way in which she treats her major subject one can see that she has chosen it not solely in order to get a degree and a well paying position later on, but because she is genuinely interested in it, because she finds intellectual enjoyment in it.

The college girl is expected to prove herself an expert in her subject, to feel thoroughly at home in it. In her concern about getting a good grade in her subject we recognize two traits: diligence and conscientiousness. If one or another girl is not naturally very intelligent, she nevertheless always proves to be a hard-working student. And she is obliged to be hard-working in order to remain in college—to be accepted by the college in the first place. Almost every day she is expected to give concrete proof of her intellectual progress. From the first day of her campus life she is caught in the stream of intellectual endeavor and she must keep on swimming tirelessly in order to be a successful college girl. One realizes that her striving for knowledge and truth is conscientious, that is, honest, and an inner compulsion soon turns it into a remarkable character trait. Any kind of sycophancy, conceit or unreasonable pride, the enticing temptation to make herself seem more than she is, all this is usually foreign to her. She knows that truth and beauty are in substance simple and genuine and that both can be accepted and assimilated only in a simple, unpretentious way. Thus we see her working on her report, her face glowing with fervor, or straining all her powers to answer examination questions, or working on a scientific experiment in the laboratory. She loves to taste ideas and to test problems.

She is so much concerned about satisfying her seeking mind that she often struggles like a work-horse.[11] "Nil sine magno labore" is her motto, and "Die Arbeit macht das Leben süss" is her consolation.[12]

In the formative process of her subjective world the teacher plays one of the most important rules. Her instructors, male and female, prepare the food of her mind and serve it to her. They are the architects of her subjective world. In classrooms, seminar rooms and laboratories she meets those who are interested in her intellectual growth. The college girl spends many hours a week with her teacher. Gradually the two get to know each other very well. They soon discover strengths and weaknesses in each other. Their mutual relationship is based on the point of view: we did not choose one another, we have been sent to one another by God in order to perform a mutual service for the mind. This service is carried out with patience, tolerance and sympathy on both sides. Both aid each other in the pursuit of the same goal, the perception of truth. The teacher is there to point out to the girl her essential problems in all clearness, and to help her solve them. The student is there to listen attentively to the problems presented and, in the process of understanding, to make them her own. She needs the teacher until she herself is able to recognize the problems and think them through.

If you want to give a small child solid food—for example, a piece of meat—you must cut the large piece into small pieces so that the child can swallow them. At the same time you must often say something funny, be tender and witty so that the unfamiliar food will taste good to the child and agree with it. This help is usually given by the child's mother, its father or older brothers or sisters. It is necessary as long as the child is not able to help itself and eat properly. A similar method is used in college where the students' intellectual fare is prepared and served to them by their teachers, their intellectual parents.

In this learning-teaching community a spirit prevails in which the original meaning of the word "study" becomes manifest. The Latin *studere* means to be alert, to be ready, to be interested, devoted, busy, industrious. It can also be explained in one phrase: "to pursue." The members of this learning-teaching community are united in their mutual pursuit of truth. Old and new problems and ideas, old and new realities are here considered, discussed, analyzed. For this purpose thick books are read and discussed, long reports are written and criticized, examinations are held, and papers are mutually corrected. In such an intellectual community of workers no one may remain passive. Even the most timid girl is called upon to speak; even the slow thinker and speaker is given an opportunity to show to what extent she has been able to follow the problem under consideration. The girl who grows tired or loses the thread is helped and put back on the right track either by one of her fellow students or by the teacher who must never grow tired or lose the thread.

Each session of such a community of workers, whether it takes place in the classroom or the laboratory, is a carefully prepared undertaking with a conscious aim, in which everyone concerned is called upon to cooperate. Sometimes this cooperation can become strenuous because it is often difficult for a girl to follow the reasoning involved. Often it requires the mobilization of all her intellectual and spiritual resources to keep pace and not act out of character, so to speak. However, the more difficult the case is, and the more concentration and reasoning power are required, the more fascinating does the girl's role become in this drama of the intellect. She becomes completely absorbed by the problem she seeks to clarify. She experiences what may be called intellectual excitement. In such a state the physical and material, the trivial and unimportant, the prosaic and humdrum—everything that is foreign to the spiritual aspect—disappear. The full force of the subjective world prevails. Then the college girl comes closer to the light of truth. Then the growth of her spirit shows a spurt, like the plant that has been freed of all weeds. It is a tense drama in which the power of the word and the force of the experiment with all its effective nuances and structures is revealed. It usually ends with the spiritual well-being of all the participants.

When the lecture, the seminar or the experiment is over, when the student and her master have slowly left the room, one sees a tenseness in their flushed faces and their eager eyes which says: "We have once more accomplished something." One feels the joy of intellectual achievement. This is confirmed if one hears them say, enthusiastically, "Once again it was superb."

Between the college girl and her professor there is often a subjective bond which can be regarded as an intellectual kinship. It is a relationship of mutual warmth and noble sympathy. Although their enthusiasm for the same subject differs in scope and depth, it brings them together. She admires his mastery of the subject, his broad view, the logic and eloquence of his words. He admires her industry and her devotion to the cause, her tireless attempt to get to the bottom of things, the way in which she strives for the cultivation of her inner world. Both remain in close contact during the work in classroom or laboratory. A friendly look, an appreciative or grateful word, an exchange of a gentle, comforting smile—all this facilitates the mutual striving and accelerates productivity. During the work period the girl's relationship to her teacher is almost like that of a singer and a conductor during a concert where, too, a reassuring look and an encouraging smile exchanged between them help them succeed.

Another source which feeds the college girl's spirit is the book. It is almost as important for the development of her subjective world as is her teacher. It is an indispensable instrument with which she builds the house of her intellect. She needs books to digest the material she gets in class, to work out a problem posed to her, to carry out her laboratory tests successfully, as well as to organize her free time in a meaningful way. The book helps her to recall what she has forgotten, to understand what has been incomprehensible, to fill in what she has left out. The book makes it possible for her to supplement and enrich the knowledge she has gained in class and in the laboratory. More than that, books are able to satisfy almost all the impulses and ambitions of her mind, to fill in all the gaps left by the teaching process. Thanks to good books, properly selected and critically read, the college girl may hope to attain the intellectual achievements which are recognized by the distinction *summa cum laude*.

Her intellectual guide, the teacher, leads her into the

realm of books and chooses for her the ones which she must study or which are useful to her, sometimes also those which relax her and give her pleasure. In the end she herself will develop good taste in her selection of the books she must read or wants to read. A taste for good books is developed slowly. It flourishes in the soil in which the inner impulses meet the outer shaping influences of her environment. One of the chief concerns of college training is to develop in the students the feeling for good books, because the college knows the quality of spiritual nourishment contained in a good book and because it knows that this spiritual food will be available to the student all her life long. "It depends on what we read," says Thomas Carlyle, "after all manner of professors have done their best for us." The college girl also realizes this and diligently practices the art of choosing good books and reading them well.

A junior confessed to her favourite high school teacher in a letter: "Presently I am in love with *The Cloak* by Gogol. Upon the suggestion of our professor of sociology I read the story and then I re-read it many times slowly and thoughtfully. Sir Francis Bacon wrote that 'some books are to be tasted, others to be swallowed, and some few to be chewed and digested.' This is one that I chew and digest; it makes me wiser. Akakiy Akakievitch, the hero of the story, cultivates my understanding of human misery and courage. He offers to me more than that. To explain this 'more,' I paraphrase here one of his daily life habits, applying it to myself: 'Having studied to my heart's content, I lie down to sleep, smiling at the thought of the coming day—of what God might send to me to learn on the morrow.' "

It is true, one does not have much benefit from a good book if one does not know how to read it properly. Reading it then becomes a waste of time. The college therefore sees to it that the student learns how to read well, that is to say, scientifically, which means thoroughly, understandingly, thoughtfully, and with a critical eye. The purpose of these exercises is to sharpen her judgment so that she will be able to distinguish easily the essential from the inessential, the distinguished from the average. Such perceptive power serves not only to make her a proper reader, but also a good writer and speaker. Therefore it is one of the chief concerns of the learner as well as the teacher to work toward competent judgment.

The intellectual nourishment which the college girl receives in the lecture room or the laboratory is prescribed and served forth in a more or less formal manner. But there are also numerous opportunities of profiting intellectually in an informal way from other servants of the mind, in other rooms and at other times of the day.[13] We refer above all to lectures and discussions which lie outside the official study program. Here the college girl often takes the opportunity to hear prominent scholars from this country and abroad, to have discussions with them, often to become personally acquainted with them and talk to them informally over a cup of tea. I remember a visit of Arnold Toynbee at a girls' college. The students grouped themselves around the scholar without any self-consciousness. One young student who was sitting on the floor asked him, "Dr. Toynbee, how did you manage to write so many books?" "I worked when I did not feel like it, and I did not work when I felt like it," replied the famous historian.

Now and then the college girl visits academic gather-

ings or meetings of student clubs where problems or ideas
are discussed or educational films are shown. Afterwards
coffee and cake are served as refreshments; sometimes there
is also music and dancing. On such occasions her psychic
and physical powers are agreeably cultivated in an indirect but effective way. They also help to break the daily
routine of classroom and library. She learns what others
are thinking and saying, and what they are doing. She
takes in much of it, talks it over with her fellow-students
and makes it her own.

Concerts, art exhibits and the theater which she visits
throughout the academic year also have an educative effect.
They, too, serve to shape her subjective world. Here those
wishes of hers which passionately demand beauty are primarily nourished. She has no difficulty seeing and appreciating the subtleties of art, for she comes from a house—
her college—where everything serves the cause of truth
and beauty, those realities which quicken the feeling of life
and which are discernible in all genuine art. Even though
she may not always be a connoisseur in the world of art,
she nevertheless always has a feeling for what the work of
art stands for, and she can enjoy it. Does she know that
this joy which releases her from everyday trifles is a fruit
of her intellectual and spiritual efforts which thrive in the
college atmosphere?

Good physical nourishment, rich in vitamins, makes the
body strong, vital and good-looking. Good, psychic nourishment, rich in ideas, makes the mind strong, creative and
fascinating. By means of good physical and mental nourishment the cultural element is developed in human beings.
This is shown in the personality of the college girl. When
one first sees her, even without knowing she is a college girl,

one feels something special in her manner, something pleasantly different that makes one think she must come from a proper, cultivated home. Dexterity of thought, elegance of expression, brilliance of wit are the characteristics which make her popular among the exacting men and women of the world. She is trained in the exercise of thought which puts her in control of the situation, she knows how to use the word "beautiful," she embodies gaiety without effort. Thus she becomes the aspiration of those who know how to appreciate the beautiful and the excellent in man.

The following incidents may make what we have just said somewhat more graphic. One of my students did her practice teaching in a high school. Since the principal of that school was well known as a strict and demanding pedagogue, I was interested in calling him up and asking how the budding teacher was getting along. "Excellent, she is excellent," he said briefly, and added, "I only hope my son, who has to do his practice teaching next year will be half as good as this young girl. Then I'll be quite satisfied."

Another student who did her practice teaching in a remote school was praised by her pupils in a letter to the editor of the local newspaper. Among other things, the pupils said: "Many of us were sorry when her teaching term was over and she had to leave. We think the students she will teach later on will be the happiest in the world."

On a train from Paris to Frankfurt I once conversed with a young American soldier. When I told him that I was teaching at a women's college in Pennsylvania he said that he had a girl friend who was a senior at a women's college in California. He showed me her picture and a recent letter that he had received from her. I read the letter and asked him for permission to copy the following lines: "Last night I finished reading *The Ugly American* and went to bed with a sour taste of American popularity abroad. I dreamed then about you—the delightful American who is warm, kind and helpful to everybody everywhere, and I waked up in high spirits."

At a women's club meeting there was to be a lecture by a well-known psychologist on the subject: "Flattery as a Psychological Phenomenon." The speaker was unable to appear. The chairman, hoping to lessen the disappointment of the audience, asked if someone present would be willing to talk about something worthwhile and interesting. A college girl got up, went to the speaker's desk and told a little story about Benjamin Franklin's youth. Once when he was a small boy, on his way to school, Benjamin Franklin met a stranger with an ax over his shoulder, who asked him whether his father had a grindstone at home, for he wanted to sharpen his ax. The stranger called little Benjamin a nice boy, which flattered the lad, so he not only led him home but fetched water for the grindstone and turned the wheel for him, although this was hard work. Meanwhile the school bell rang, but the boy kept on turning the wheel because the ax was not yet sharp enough and, after all, the stranger had called him a fine, strong boy. Finally, when the ax was sharp enough the stranger suddenly began to scold the youth: "You lazybones, what are you doing here, hurry up and get to school!" Benjamin Franklin never forgot this experience, and later whenever anyone wanted to flatter him, he said to himself: "Watch out, this man has an ax to grind!"

The audience was enchanted, not only with the story,

which vividly illustrated the background of flattery, but especially with the striking way in which the college girl presented it. People were also surprised when she mentioned that she had first read this story in her German reader.

A dainty, slightly built college girl stood at the cashier's desk beside the entrance to the campus concert hall. People from out of town had also been invited, so that there were many students from neighboring colleges. One of these students, an athletic type, suddenly placed his hand on the money in the cardboard box, as though to snatch it like a delinquent. In a flash the dainty little girl seized the young man by the collar and said jokingly, "Now I know why the college got the strongest girl on the campus to act as cashier."

During a Latin class the professor explained the phrase *panem et circenses* (bread and circus) and asked the students to translate the well-known quotation into American. "Hot dogs and baseball!" was their very apt translation.

"Problems, problems," shouted a sophomore during a bull session, "in every class! And here we are, expected to solve all the problems. If we solve all the problems, what will our kids do? They will get bored to death."

These examples, which could be multiplied many times, reflect the college girl's subjective world, equipped with knowledge and practical knowhow, and adorned with wit and elegant repartee.

To the eye of the keen observer, many of her acts, in her struggle for self-realization, appear in her milieu as sparks of "aesthetic bliss." One cannot but notice the marvelous and original human gestures that rise from the controlled mind and the examined heart. They affect you like verses that give both delight and wisdom.

Her Relation to Herself and Others

Being sweet—always, but not too sweet.

The outer and inner world of a person can be treated separately only in theory and for the purpose of psychological, sociological or esthetic analysis. In reality both are an inseparable organic unity known as the personality. The personality, in turn, manifests itself in the way a human being reacts to himself and his environment. It is therefore logical that one must observe a person's relation to the world around him if one wishes to have a clear picture of his personality.

Since it is our aim to obtain as accurate a picture as possible of the personality of the college girl, we shall attempt in this chapter to describe her relation to herself, her fellowmen, to God and nature. In the preceding pages we have already touched upon her relation to these phenomena; now we shall go into more detail.

Her relation to herself can best be explained on the basis of the name "college girl" which she bears. To begin with, this name tells us the following: she is a girl who, after successful completion of high school, has been accepted by a higher institution of learning, is studying there for a degree which will entitle her to a professional position or, as people often say, will enable her to meet a young man in good circumstances and marry him. But this is a purely external explanation which by no means exhausts the meaning of the term "college girl." The designation "college girl" also says this: she is a young woman who, over a period of four years, grows up in an elevated atmosphere, who thinks clearly, speaks attractively, dresses tastefully, has good manners—in short, is a truly well-bred girl in whose presence one feels the splendor of human life.

The college girl becomes aware of this meaning of the term even in the first few weeks of her campus life. In her new environment she is shown a new personality, she sees what she must become, how her parents and relatives, her friends and acquaintances, in fact, even strangers wish to see her. Trying to emulate this picture of the college girl causes her concern, but also gives her satisfaction. It obligates her first of all to work attentively on herself. This means unfolding the tendencies and characteristics which ennoble her being and regulate her behavior. Consciously or unconsciously, willingly or unwillingly, she must always observe herself critically. Her thinking is trained, her speech polished, her self-control sharpened. The movements of her body become almost intuitively more attractive, her taste in clothes becomes authoritative. She works indefatigably on herself in order to do justice to the responsibility implicit in her name. Moreover, she is intelligent enough to know that a college girl and *the* college girl are not one and the same. She is aware that there are various levels of quality. But she takes seriously this unique and perhaps decisive opportunity to shape her life, in order to make something superior out of it.

Though the work of self-education may be bitter, the fruits to be gathered from it are sweet. The college girl is as happy as a child over any progress, no matter how small, in the development of character or intellect. Once a student showed me her chemistry examination paper marked "Very good." She had put it in a frame which she had painstakingly made herself. The grade came from a professor who was widely known as being rather demanding in his field. Enthusiastically she explained to me, "This is the first time in two years that I got this grade. I'm overjoyed!" I know of another case where a college girl was so happily excited that she forgot her lunch on receiving a letter from the president of a church group who named her the queen of the last rose festival and praised her particularly for her simple yet very attractive gown. Thus the college girl is concerned about every step that brings her closer to the perfection of her personality, for it is evidence of that progress which is changing her life.

One of her greatest concerns, if not *the* greatest encountered in her relation with herself is her anxiety to achieve a balance between her inner and her outer world, between the consideration of her intellectual powers and the cultivation of her physical appearance. Each is important for her, for they are both component parts of her essential personality. Both are primary elements which confirm and strengthen the title "college girl." Thus she is called upon to make sure that the inner world is not neglected in favor of the outer, and vice versa. A cultivated body and a cultivated soul belong together to complete the personality picture. She knows this, for she has experienced it within herself. If outwardly she appears immaculately groomed but inwardly rather inferior, she feels inhibited and uncomfortable. If she excels in intellectual matters but outwardly neglects herself and appears unkempt, she also feels uncomfortable and strange. But if she appears in the splendor of her intellectual and physical cultivation she immediately feels at home, at ease and content. This goal alone embodies her noble endeavor. It also concretely expresses the meaning of the term "college girl."

It should not be supposed that the harmony between a cultivated inner and outer world is easy to attain. It is not only on special occasions that she must present and sustain a distinguished appearance, but always, even at the most unimportant private as well as official functions. It is true, such an appearance seems a fascinating game, and the one who benefits from it thinks it is simple and natural, achieved without apparent difficulty or effort. It looks as though it were inevitable, as though this were her true nature. Every talented and trained actress gives this impression, no matter whether her stage is that of the theatre or of life. Only the initiated know how much time and trouble it costs the actress as well as her directors to ensure success.

In this connection we must also mention the fact that there are many college girls who never manage to become the persons they should be. They fail to exemplify the distinguished meaning of the title college girl. Others succeed only to a certain extent. Both the one who fails and the one who is only partially successful obviously have difficulty in their association with themselves and in finding their way about in the higher educational process. In general their numbers are few, too few to darken the glowing picture of the college girl who lives up to that name.

In her successful association with herself, which includes above all the cultivation of inner and outer abilities and their harmonious expression, the college girl builds a character based on self-confidence and integrity. It is the core of her personality. She develops a talent for grasping the given situation and mastering it and this gives her self-confidence. Her ability to make other people aware of beauty through her attitude, and to be genuine and natural about it, makes her confident and at the same time unique. For these qualities which have grown out of the campus atmosphere and in the process of her development in college she is widely admired, cared for and possibly loved. These qualities are probably also the reason for her pride and her self-contentment. Pride in this case, however, does not mean haughtiness, or egotism or selfishness. This would be false. Haughtiness and selfishness are foreign to her nature. She is proud of herself because she is aware of her dignity as a college girl. She is pleased with herself because she has achieved something which seems valuable and beautiful in her eyes and in the eyes of others. That is why she is pleased to be a college girl—a title of which she can be proud.

Another striking point in her relation to herself is the mood of not-yet. While she is endeavoring to coördinate her inner and outer abilities she finds herself in a mood of waiting, of not-yet. Curiosity and anticipation, longing and expectation, irritability and impatience are elements of this mood. The college girl is curious about herself. She is anxious to see what will become of her here in college and later in life. She has her own ideas and plans which she longs to see realized. With great interest she awaits the outcome of her plans. She would like to see results as soon as possible. She becomes impatient and almost irritable when she thinks of a future phase of her life, either an important examination, a promising date, her first job after her final examination or her engagement party. These and other scenes pass before her vision and entice her to play the game. But the time has not yet come when she can play her part, when she can show her ability for her own enjoyment and that of others—not today, not yet.

This not-yet creates a mood in her which stimulates her as wine might do. She is pleasantly excited and stimulated and in turn stimulates those around her. This mood of elation nourished and activated by the mood of not-yet, can also be described as enthusiasm which brings about an increased feeling of life. Her whole being is imbued with this enthusiastic mood of not-yet. Her expression, the sound of her voice, the movement of her hands—her entire attitude betrays this particular feeling. True, other young girls who are not college girls are also more or less sustained by this mood. But it arises from another source and leads to other goals. Moreover, the way she gives herself and the impression she awakens are different.

The college girl's relation to herself also essentially determines her relation to others.

Young, cultivated inwardly as well as outwardly, open and gay, self-confident and at the same time modest, hopeful and enthusiastic—that is the way you find the college girl when you meet her. She is not insistent when she asks you for something or requests something. She is grateful for the little things granted her. She is not offended if you look at her with critical eyes, and she does not laugh at you contemptuously if you do or say something stupid. If you praise her, she is confused and blushes. If she praises you, you have the feeling that she is sincere. If you are in difficulties, she will be the first to give you a word of advice and a helping hand, without expecting your "thank you." If she is in difficulty and you help her, she accepts your help as a great gift. And you are amazed by her capacity to remain cheerful and controlled in situations where others weep, or explode into hysterics, or sweat and complain. You observe her from the side: how she is dressed, how she moves, how she speaks or laughs; you see her personal style in the way she goes about her work or drinks her coffee. Finally you discover that her very presence leaves an impression of taste and intelligence. And when you no longer see the college girl you are left with a picture of her that has involuntarily impressed itself upon you and cannot be removed.

The reaction of the college girl toward other people, and their reaction to her, is above all a mutually happy exchange. The fact that this is so can be most clearly seen in her relation to her parents and others who are close to her. She has become more mature. She is separated from her home. This gives her the possibility of appreciating her home more. Now she has also become better able to understand her parents. She knows how much time, effort and money they have sacrificed and are still sacrificing in order to give her the best possible education, in order to equip her beautifully for a beautiful life. She also knows the ideal picture which her parents have of her: she is supposed to be diligent and industrious, noble and helpful —a good student and a good girl at the same time. She makes a serious effort to let the wishful image of her parents come true, for after all it coincides with the idealistic image she herself has of her personality. She would not like to disappoint her parents and herself.

A student once seemed somewhat discontented as she looked at her corrected examination paper in Greek, marked "Good." When the teacher tried to discover the reason for her ill-humor, she said that she aimed to get "Very good" in Greek because this would not only satisfy *her* but above all her father who was convinced that the Greek language was a language of wisdom and beauty.

It is not only in her studies that she tries to please her parents. On every suitable occasion she is an attentive and grateful child, capable and willing to do something, even without their help, to make them happy.

One Saturday morning I boarded the bus which goes from the campus into town. I met a student who said she was going to work. "Must you work?" I asked astonished, for I knew that she came from a well-to-do family. "My father has a birthday soon," she explained, "and I want to buy him a nice present, so I am working every Saturday now." Then she added, "Of course my mother sent me extra money for his present, but I shan't use that. I would rather buy my father a present with the money I have earned myself."

Here is another incident which seems pertinent in this context, and shows that the college girl can give pleasure to her whole family. One day in the library a college girl discovered an anthology of poems by French children. One little poem, especially, attracted her attention: "Dear Mama, you know that I like you. If I were a bird I would fly into the trees and sing for your pleasure. If I were a miner I would dig deep into the earth. I would have gold to make you beautiful, dear Mama." She thought this poem by an eight-year-old so adorable that she immediately copied it and learned it by heart. Finally she had the idea of teaching it to her little brother in French. On her mother's birthday, when all the relatives and guests were assembled, the little boy said, "I have a present for you, too, Mama." Then he recited the poem to everybody's delight.

The college girl's relationship to her family is one of mutual enrichment. That is the intelligent meaning of family to the college girl and her meaning to the family. Both help each other and grow in happiness which is primarily spiritual.

The college girl thoroughly appreciates the fact that her family wants to take good care of her, keep her healthy, clothe her adequately, see to it that she studies diligently and is content. She is glad of this. But it is a pleasure that requires two things. First of all, gratitude. Neither her parents nor her relatives who are helping her owe her anything. They have done enough for her and have made enough sacrifices in bringing her up. She knows that other girls of her age are left to their own devices and must get along without help from home and without a higher education. Thus she accepts this solicitude as a valuable gift. The second requirement is action. She is given four years in which to educate and cultivate herself. This is a unique opportunity. She urgently wishes to make good use of this opportunity—to obtain during this period the insight which will lead her to an intelligent and happy life. This insight gives her such joy that she is driven on to greater and deeper discernment.

Whenever the college girl is with her family she draws

them into her world. She tells them about her instructors and her books, about her academic and social activities, about her failures and successes, her worries and joys, her newly discovered friends, both male and female. She vividly describes what she has already accomplished, what is still to be accomplished, in short, what she is and what she can yet become. Thus she draws a complex picture of herself, which in many cases is a source of joy to her family. "Their" college girl makes them recall their happiest memories of youth. Often their college girl rouses them out of their mental lethargy. In her they see fulfilled many of their unsatisfied wishes. Thus the meeting between the college girl and her mother, her father or one of her relatives is more than a mere reunion. It is a gratifying experience which brings much joy.

One spring day I met a girl on the campus and together we admired the grounds and the trees that were showing their first green. The student mentioned that at home they also had a large garden. "Then you have plenty to do during summer vacation," I observed. "My father does most of it," she said. "Taking care of the garden is his hobby. But when I am at home he likes me to be near him, which I often am."

To the initiated, that is, to one who has an opportunity to observe the college girl's relationship with her parents, this direct and open feeling between a father and his daughter is not by any means an exception or a rarity. Another two or three years and her parents will not see her so often, so young, fresh and gay. After her graduation she will either marry soon or take some position. She will be living her own life and will inure herself against life's storms. The college girl vaguely feels this. Perhaps that is also one of the reasons for the cordial relationship filled with warmth and sympathy between her and her parents. Those who love each other and see an imminent parting gently assure each other every minute of their presence together and are glad that they can still see, hear and speak to one another.

Besides her parents and relatives the person which the college girl meets most often is her fellow-student. In class, in the library, in the dining hall, on the campus sport grounds, in all the dormitory rooms the two meet. They have the same privileges and duties. Both have the same daily routine, take part in the same celebrations, and are more or less dependent on each other. This teaches the college girl to get along peaceably with her neighbor, to understand and respect her. In her daily contact with her fellow-students she also has many opportunities to become better acquainted with herself. She observes, compares, asks questions. In this way she learns much that was unfamiliar to her. Her relationship to her fellow-students rests on tolerance, humor and helpful understanding. The following cases will show what the students can mean to one another.

In one of my classes I had two students who profited a great deal from each other. One of them had an obvious tendency to nervousness. The slightest failure unnerved her, although she was very keen and quick-witted. The other girl was quiet and serene, but less intelligent. Her perseverance and decisiveness were an indispensable example to the first girl from whose sound and brilliant insights the other, in turn, profited. Outside of class, too, they were good friends. Another case: Two roommates soon discovered their chief weaknesses which made their life together rather annoying. One of them was untidy, the other had the habit of talking too much about herself. They made their failings known to each other in the following way. On the desk of the untidy girl there appeared one day the Latin dictum: "Serva ordinem et ordo te servabit" (Serve order and order will serve you). The next day the girl who was always glorifying herself found the following German proverb on her desk: "Eigenlob stinkt!" (Vainglory stinks).

The following case also shows what a beneficial effect a college community can have. A very intelligent and clever student was shy and rather unsure of herself, especially if she had to appear or speak in public. At a student meeting she was nominated and elected president of her class. The confidence of her fellow-students gave her courage and self-confidence. At the end of the year she was honored by her grateful class with a gift for her excellent leadership. "I owe my success to all of you; I am very happy," she said in her farewell speech. It was true.

Community life on the campus means that one gives and at the same time acquires polish. In the cafeteria, on the stage and on the sport grounds, at informal and formal parties which the girls give among themselves, the college girl entertains her fellow-students and is entertained by them. They joke, laugh and sing together, stimulated by the same mood. One class will arrange a festive dinner or a dance in honor of another class. Thus they entertain each other in different clothes, under different lights, in other rooms and in another state of mind. For a short time the college girl forgets books and teachers. In a refreshing atmosphere she enjoys the faces familiar to her which now appear in a new light. Ceremonious, albeit minor occasions,

alter her routine and she, too, is changed to her own delight and that of her companions. At the end of the
school year farewell celebrations are held for the
graduates. On this occasion those who are leaving and
those who are staying meet to thank each other for the
happiness they have given each other, and once again
vow eternal friendship. These are moments when college
girls part in a mood of deep affection and well-wishing.

In her association with her fellow-students on the
campus the college girl acquires an admirable style in
human contacts—a social style which manifests itself not
as something borrowed but as something attained.

It is in a spirit of mutual understanding and esteem that
the college girl and her instructor meet on the campus.
Together they experience depths and heights in their
common devotion to the mind. Both struggle for understanding in the things that are still unfamiliar to them,
for clarification of problems which are still not clear. Day
after day both are concerned about the results of their
striving. They both work hard, often to the point of ex-
haustion; but they jest in order to relieve the strain of the
class, work again, grow tired again, and wait for vacation.
Mutual work and mutual striving unite strangers and
make them friends. In the same way the tie is formed
between the college girl and her teacher, and this, it
should be emphasized, is based on cordial attentiveness and
sensitive tact.

They become acquainted not only intellectually but also
in a human way. The teacher thinks about her even outside the classroom. He congratulates her on her success
as a public speaker, a singer, an actress, an author, or the
captain of her hockey team. She does not neglect to

mention his newly published essay or his book that has just come out. He occasionally inquires about her family, and she about his children.

If he sometimes finds that she is a bit sad or out of sorts, he always finds an encouraging word for her, such as, "Tomorrow you'll see things in a different light." And he must not be annoyed with her if sometimes in passing she says something in a cordial, gay voice, something inconsequentially flattering, such as, "I like your new tie."

One day in the campus dining hall, strawberry shortcake was served at lunch. A philosophy professor remarked to his colleagues, "It's delicious, I wish there were more." A student sitting at the next table heard this. She got up, took her portion of strawberry shortcake and offered it to the professor, saying, "This is for your wise answer to my question in class this morning."

It often happens that she will say to a teacher, especially one whom she knows very well, "If you ever come to my home town, please visit us. I would love to have you meet my family." She also invites him to family gatherings and parties of friends. If he is ill she brings him flowers, even though she may be bored to death in his class.

Another example of her close friendship with her teacher is shown in the case of a teacher, who for some reason was obliged to give up his position at a college and was unable immediately to find another. The students took up a collection which made it possible for him and his family to get along for a time.

The drama on the stage of the intellect is played on both sides with mutual respect and delicate sensitivity.

The relationship between teacher and student is thus raised to a higher human level. Two events illustrate this.

During a lesson one student repeatedly asked questions. When class was over she went up to the teacher and said, "Please forgive me, Professor, for asking so many questions. I am afraid I held up the class work."

Another time it happened that in reprimanding an inattentive student the teacher raised his voice. The student felt hurt and broke into tears. As a result, the atmosphere in the classroom became somewhat oppressive. The teacher was well aware of it and shortly before the end of the lesson he said quietly to the girl, "I did not mean to offend you. Please forgive me if my voice sounded as though I did." Her tearful eyes immediately cleared; she smiled. It was a relieved, conciliatory smile, a relief for her and for everyone present.

Just as the teacher does not have the same regard for all students, so the student does not like all her teachers equally well. This is obvious, and there are many reasons for it. We shall not go into them, for this problem is not pertinent to our consideration. But the following must be mentioned. All factual and personal problems which now and then arise between the college girl and her teacher are usually solved to the advantage of both without great difficulty and without much friction. In the process, both gain in their mastery of the subject and of life. The very spirit of the college demands understanding and mutually helpful cooperation. Both are called upon to cultivate their intellect and nurture their soul, that is, to exalt the human aspect.

True service of the spirit can at times produce an exceptionally fine relationship between a student and her master. Once when a college girl heard that one of her professors was retiring and would not teach the following autumn, she wrote him a letter in which she thanked him for his excellent teaching. The letter concluded: "If you are no longer here I really do not know from whom I shall learn so much. You taught by suggesting rather than by dogmatizing, and each time after your class I had the wish to teach myself and to teach others the way you did." The aged professor replied: "I did not know that I meant so much to you. I always had the feeling, and I still have it, that I learned more from you than I was able to teach you. Many of your questions were a challenge to my thinking, and the original forms of your benign behavior enriched my appreciation of humanity."

During holidays and during mid-term vacation the college girl now and then meets her instructor on the athletic field, in the theatre, or when she goes shopping. They are both glad to meet. Usually they greet one another and talk. But even if the casual meeting consists of only a friendly "Good day," both are inevitably reminded of the hours spent together in academic surroundings.

Besides her parents, relatives, fellow-students and teachers, there is one other person who plays no little part in a girl's life during her college days. That is her boy friend. Just as her parents and teachers are absolutely necessary to the shaping of her life, so, with almost the same urgency, she needs such a friend. He, too, is necessary to shape and round out her personality. Once I overheard the following conversation between the head of a dormitory and a student. "Aren't you going to the ball tonight?" "No, not this time." "No escort?" "Oh yes, my friend would like to go, but I told him that this time I do not want to go out." "Why?" "I have to prepare a paper for English, and besides I have to write a letter to my parents." "You can finish your paper later, and I'm sure your parents can wait a day longer for your letter, but you ought not to give up your date for tonight. You know it's a ball that takes place only once a year. You must meet new people, new men. Every opportunity is valuable. Besides, the change will do you good. I would advise you to call up your friend and tell him that you have changed your plans and want to go after all." The experienced, dignified-looking dormitory mother spoke simply and convincingly.

The advice to go to a dance rather than to study or write to one's family may sound strange at first. But a thoughtful person will find it very sensible. The girl's studies will soon be over; then she will probably leave her parental home and follow her husband, as the Bible says. She must find this man, which means she must know him thoroughly, compare him with others, test him, learn his strength and his weakness. If he is not the right man for her she must give him up and look for another, one who has been "sent by God." But the one sent by God wants to be found, and even if he is near at hand, to be discovered by her as the right one. She must undoubtedly use every opportunity for this.

Many college girls become engaged during their student days, especially in the last two years. Some marry on the day of graduation, others immediately after, many later. There are only a few who remain unmarried for a longer period or who never marry. Statistics show that divorce is much rarer in marriages between college people than in marriages between a couple who have never attended college. This is a great honor for the college girl who knows how to choose the right one and get along with him.[14]

In the simple little world in which the college girl moves, her boy friend has an important place. She gives him a great deal of her time. She dreams about him and talks about him, writes to him and goes out with him. Her attitude toward him when she is with him, privately or in public, reveals aspects of her character and the results of her education.

We have already pointed out that the college girl is an actress. As a matter of fact, everyone acts, no matter what his role on life's stage. With the college girl there is a difference. She is as a rule spared the tragic roles which others must often perform. It is a gay and tranquil play that goes on before her, somewhat lighter than an opera but more meaningful than an operetta. It is gayer than a drama, but gentler than a comedy. It has little to do with the elements of tragedy. It is a play by itself which does not yet have a name, probably because it is rather new.

Her performance at home with her parents is characterized by cordiality and respect; in class with teachers it shows devotion and aspiration; with her friends and acquaintances we discover humor and cleverness. On the dance floor with her boy friend her performance is a mixture of enjoyment and intelligence. This we must examine.

At most of the social events which the college girl attends there is dancing. She dances at formal balls and at informal gatherings, in large brilliantly lit rooms and under the soft lights of a small night club somewhere at the edge of town. She dances publicly to the festive music of a large orchestra, and privately to the sounds of a disc. She dances classic and dignified dances, as well as wild and provocative dances. She dances during the college term and during vacation. After all, she cannot always study, ponder intellectual problems, or nourish her mind. She has not only a mental life, but also a physical one. She needs a change during which she can also nourish her senses in a seemly way. She cannot always live on intellectual and spiritual stimulation. She needs emotional excitement, too. Dancing gives her an excellent opportunity for this.

During her study she experiences intellectual excitement; during dancing an enjoyable excitement of the senses. The way she behaves and the way she handles her partner during the dance which is often tempting, is characteristic of her and at the same time significant. The striking thing you discern in her behavior on the dance floor is self-control. She needs this in order to remain herself; that is to say, to keep her spiritual and physical equilibrium amid the enticing tones of the music, the romantic whispered endearments of her partner. With it all she remains flexible—flexible in her feelings and in her movements. She must be that in order to fulfill the meaning of the dance, in order to give herself and her partner the slight, though brief pleasure derived from exploring one another, cautiously and in moderation.

In her flexibility as in her enjoyment she is, however, always aware of limits. This awareness protects the dancing girl from infractions and excesses, yet does not prevent her from putting herself into the mood of the music and of her partner and of responding to them. It tells her how high she may lift her feet, how loudly she may sing the words of the song hit, to what extent she may follow her dancing partner in his daring and acrobatic improvisations. It almost intuitively regulates her body and the way she holds her hands. It estimates the extent to which her body may yield and comply and at the same time harmoniously balance the movements of her partner with her own. In this awareness of limits the dancers enjoy each other without offending dignity and tact.

Holding hands and embracing in the dance tempts the dancers to play the game of love. She plays along and conducts herself like a dancing artist—physical contact, yes, but scarcely noticeable; cheek to cheek—certainly, but not too long; stroking her friend's hair a bit—why not, but almost imperceptibly; being sweet—always, but not too sweet! All this shows her subtle sense of distance within proximity. Thanks to this attitude, her love play in the dance is elegant and admirable and at the same time protects her from excesses. Thus the dance becomes not "sexual intercourse to music," to quote a German professor of music, but an enchanting play imbued with warmth and gaiety, which she may share with the one whom she likes.

The game of love which she and her friend enjoy at dances or on other occasions is kindled, kept alive and intensified by her original fancies. Her childlike, yielding attitude, her kindly look, her roguish smile, her humorous words, her warm handshake are all graceful little gestures of love which enchant her admirer. Anyone who is a match for this type of love play and really knows how to enter into it is put into a mood that can only be expressed in the words: "Linger, thou moment!"

Her sensitive feeling for the subtle helps her grasp the

spirit of the situation and act accordingly. It dictates to her what is proper here and now, and what is improper. If necessary, she can change herself from a young lady into a wild Indian girl. Once, on a transatlantic liner, a college girl danced rock-'n-roll until far into the night. She was dressed in a short white dress, her skin was deeply tanned, she wore a little feather in her hair. In the middle of the dance her shoes annoyed her, so she kicked them off and one of the shoes broke a window in the cabin. When the wild dance was over, she went to the corner table at which the ship's officers were sitting and excused herself. "Never mind," said the captain, "we enjoyed it." Then he ordered the waiter to bring a bottle of champagne to the table of the dancing girl. The next day when I saw the same girl at the lunch table I was pleasantly surprised. She sat there, calm, collected and ladylike. Because she had spent herself, one might say. No, it seems more true to say, because she had a subtle sense of time and place.

In her association with the young man who is her friend and whom she likes, her art of love is demonstrated. It consists primarily of inventiveness in the nuances of the game. Her ability to be inventive may, in turn, be traced to the subtlety of her cultivated feeling. A girl with a dull, undeveloped mind remains boring even in her love play. This will scarcely ever be the case with the college girl unless she has not had enough sleep or is facing a difficult examination. She waves to him when she leaves him. She says, "I am happy to be with you again," when she sits down beside him. She amuses him with stories about the audacity of her little brother, or about amusing ideas of her teacher, about gay incidents on her last shopping trip in town. Then she lets her carefully cared-for hands speak for a change, as she embraces him gently, lovingly; as she carefully lifts her glass to his lips, touches his tie, barely perceptibly; or simply reaches for his hands, unconsciously seeking. If he tells her something, she listens like a child who is being told a fairy tale. If he squeezes her hand, she smiles at him and pinches the corners of her eyes together like a little elf who has discovered something pleasing. In a hundred little ways and nuances she entertains her lover and charms him with her magic.

Through her spirited, inventive and highly sensitive coöperation in the game of love she renders a twofold service, to herself and her partner. They are both prevented from succumbing to the demands of baser instincts, and their mutual respect is increased and transformed into a higher type of longing. If her partner is not equal to the love game or wants to go too far, he is promptly dismissed. As a matter of fact, he usually leaves the field of his own accord to avoid the humiliation of exposing his immaturity in the presence of a person who expects chivalrous, manly behavior on his part. If such a young man thinks about it he will not regret what has happened, for it teaches him that even in the intoxication of love there are unwritten laws which one must observe in order to keep love alive and let it grow.

If the college girl goes out with her friend for a short evening or for a whole weekend, if she spends the time in public or private places, if her good-night kiss sometimes lasts until three in the morning, she will always remain what she truly is—dignified and charming. Everything that happens to her day or night should happen in such a way that she may laugh the next morning as only a child can laugh.

There is a popular song in which the girl begs her lover: "Keep away from college girls." The suppliant, herself not a college girl, knows that she cannot compare herself with a college girl. She feels she cannot command the adroit social behavior natural to a college girl, which will fascinate the young man.

In her association with people who are neither relatives nor intimate friends, the college girl is always gracious and helpful. Because she herself lives in happiness and strives to increase it, she is interested in having other people happy and contented, even people she does not know, whom she meets casually. She knows that her happiness can be real and enduring only if others can also be happy. Hence she meets everyone in a spirit of true friendliness and helpfulness. A clergyman whom I once visited in a girls' college remarked about the students, "They are not all intellectual stars, but they are all friendly and helpful to everyone." This conclusion was the result of his years of experience in the service of the college girl.

She is mature enough to be able to recognize sorrow and care in human beings even if she herself has as yet been spared these trials. She is always ready and willing to alleviate suffering, to relieve someone of worry, to reach out a helping hand, give a consoling look to one who is sad. Insofar as she has time and opportunity she always takes an active part where human beings need help and kindliness in order to be happy again. You can see with what friendliness she greets a workman on the campus, even though she does not know him; with what solicitude she helps an old woman off a bus; how soothingly she talks to a small boy she happens to meet who is crying; how, during vacation, she listens with patient understanding to the long-winded stories of a neighbor over the fence. She treats people she meets with an open heart and loving attentiveness.

In her gay, helpful attitude the college girl has a refreshing and positive effect on other people. The deep kindliness which is visible in her features, her sensitivity in action have a constructive influence on her environment. Life is lived by her in a more beautiful form, and her fellowmen are called upon to follow her example. For her part, in her association with others, she learns those small, instinctive bits of worldly wisdom which are not found in books but which have crystallized in the daily life of simple people. In mutual enrichment she creates for herself and others a life that gives out more vitality and joy.

The American college girl was born, grows up and studies in a country whose motto is: "In God we trust!" Although this motto does not mean much to many in this divinely favored land, nevertheless, by and large, it has a deep significance for the college girl. We realize this in her religious feeling, expressed in her view of life and her attitude toward life. She knows that she is considerably more than a "better animal." She is aware of her inner yearning toward God. She reaches out to God, though she does not always do so consciously or directly. Who, after all, does?

In a country where there is religious freedom she has many possibilities, both on and off the campus, to think about God and to revere Him in her own way. For one girl this will be more, for another, less. Much depends on the place given to religion in the family atmosphere in her home, and what her religion or her Christian denomination is. It is, however, rare to find a girl who is indifferent toward the worship of God in some form, either conventional or liberal. Usually she takes part in religious services in the campus chapel. During vacation one also sees her going to church on Sunday. She sings in the choir and helps the pastor in activities for the children. She is active in church societies and gives alms to the poor. She attends church affairs and sells lottery tickets for the benefit of African missions.

One Saturday evening late in the fall, I met one of my students standing in the cold and rain waiting for a bus. "Where in the world are you going in this miserable weather?" I asked, astonished. "To the hospital. I go there every Saturday evening." "To work?" I asked. "Yes, if you can call it that. I do one or two hours of volunteer work entertaining children who are stricken with polio."

By chance I also once saw an old rabbi and two college girls in the auditorium of a Jewish community center laboring over packages of used clothing which were being sent to refugees in Israel.

By doing work which alleviates the misery of the world and increases its joy the college girl fulfills the will of God on earth. This manifests her relationship to God. The spirit which grows out of her fervent relationship to God penetrates her personality and is reflected in the sparkle of her eyes. Even the girl who does not believe in God and does not bother about her soul's immortality—a case one does not often meet in the American girls' college—unconsciously serves God by consciously doing what is good. She unconsciously searches for Him by consciously striving for beauty. Her face, too, betrays the image of the divine.

The college girl is closely united not only with God and

with human beings, but also with nature. In its beauty she discovers signs of God. She loves to walk or drive into the country, whether on a picnic or a short excursion. When she has an opportunity she rides horseback through the woods to enjoy the pure air. She travels into the mountains to go skiing and to be alone with sun and snow. In the spring she admires the delicate buds, and in the fall she takes time out to see the autumn colors of the leaves. During vacation she tends the flowers around the house of her parents, as though her happiness and that of her whole family depended upon this.

On a voyage to Europe I happened to have a conversation with a college girl. She was looking forward to seeing Italy because she had heard that the sky was so clear and blue there one could sometimes see the stars even in daytime. She also told me that she wanted to swim in Lake Constance because the water was said to be clearer, purer and more fragrant than anywhere else in the world. She also told me that she expected to go to Brazil before long, that there was a flower there called La Mudadera. In the morning it blossoms white, at noon, red, and in the evening, dark. She had a hankering to see this strange flower.

On the same voyage I noticed another college girl who very much enjoyed watching and trying to photograph the flying fish dancing on the waves. She was sad if a day went by on which she did not see a flying fish. An old sailor told her that some fish dance on the water at sunrise. She gave the cabin steward a tip to waken her before sunrise. Soon everybody on the ship knew about her passion. One day in the ship's newspaper there appeared an illustration: an elegant girl with a camera held up to her eyes and many fish dancing on the waves. The picture bore the caption: "A lucky moment for Agnes."

Many beauties of nature which people often take for granted and to which they pay no attention awaken a great interest in the heart of the college girl, simply because she knows how to see and capture beauty for herself. When she looks at a rose or a rainbow she experiences a feeling which alters the commonplace. This explains her deep union with the beautiful things of nature and of her environment.

If the heart of human relationship is love, then it must be noted that the love of the college girl embraces both the body and the spirit of the person who happens to be loved by her; and again she expects in her own heart to be loved as a whole person. This principle is valid for her even in the highly intimate moments of love. It would mean to her a sin against her sense of dignity, educated taste, and cultivated grace to allow herself to be dominated by the lower senses alone, in all the situations of love. Awareness of that makes her superior to all those who fall in love only with the young, handsome, and warm body of their counterpart. She is always delighted if she discovers some light of the soul, *vivida vis animi,* in another person. Her satisfaction is great if another person discovers the same in her.

If a situation arises in which she disagrees with somebody—friend, neighbor, teacher or relative—her disagreement is calm, almost friendly, accompanied by terse humor. Practice in fellowship, built on cordial tolerance, appears to be one (a special one) of her extracurricular activities. As a result, her relations to herself and others (human beings, animals, and things) are based upon her sense of the right distance. She is delighted and brings delight, because she is not too far and not too close, just in the right "place"; sometimes she may be marginal, never, as a rule, beyond the limits, never a slave of excess. Her sense of the right distance, however, becomes more impressive if we face her as an inwardly and outwardly cultivated person.

The Cultivated Soul in the Cultivated Body

Her goal is to live in beauty and dignity.

The Greek ideal was a beautiful, cultivated body and a virtuous soul. Today we still seek a beautiful soul in a beautiful body. Even in beauty contests where, unfortunately, the structure of the body is, as a rule, the decisive factor, the judges now and then also consider the superior character traits of the applicant.

The classic image of the human form which the ancient Greeks longed for is today exemplified to a large extent in the American college girl. Even if her natural physical endowment does not always correspond to beauty queen standards, she nevertheless gives an impression of beauty because her body is tastefully and stylishly groomed. She has time to do this with modern means. Although by nature she is not always very gifted, she nevertheless radiates goodness, for this is carefully cultivated and bred in her by the successful application of new methods. The result is a human image which in character and expression creates a classic effect because a cultivated soul dwells in a cultivated body.

The following lines from the diary of a college girl demonstrate what was just stated:

"Right after dinner I sat down at the piano in the living room to play for half an hour as usual. I was interrupted. Kay (a fellow student) told me that Fred (her boy friend) was waiting for me in the reception room. I went to my room because I was not sure whether I was presentable. I quickly did my hair and washed my hands. I was about to go down when it occurred to me that I'd better put on another dress, the one Mother and Daddy gave me for my birthday, which Fred had not yet seen. So I quickly changed. In the reception room Fred stood talking to Miss Feeney, our dormitory mother. He was smoking. I didn't care for that. Miss Feeney doesn't like smokers, especially young men who smoke in her presence. I greeted them both and at an opportune moment I took Fred's cigarette out of his hand and put it out. Miss Feeney politely said, 'But why? It's quite permissible to smoke here.' Fred did not say anything; he understood my gesture. Then we all sat down and talked for a while. When I said that I had just been playing Haydn we started to talk about him. Miss Feeney wondered why I liked Haydn. I said I thought Haydn had the ability of putting something serious in gay form, and to illustrate this I added, 'Once when Haydn was asked why he put happy melodies into his Masses, he is said to have replied that he could not be sad when he thought about God. Goethe was supposed to have wept when Eckermann told him this.' Fred remarked that Santayana called Goethe the wisest among humans. 'It is wonderful to meet young people here; one always learns something new,' Miss Feeney said as she got up to go. I was glad to hear that, for she always means what she says."

This page from a diary reveals the taste and tact of the college girl. Three basic harmonious traits of her nature are clearly shown here. The fact that she changes her dress shows her concern for the cultivation of her appearance. Her remembering the words of Haydn shows her exquisite taste in the enrichment of her inner world. The episode of Fred's cigarette points to her tact in carrying on social intercourse that will be pleasing to all the persons involved. Her cultivated taste and tact are "wonderful," that is, classic, for one always learns "something new" from her.

This example, taken from a diary, illustrates a cultivated soul in a cultivated body, and is characteristic of *the* American college girl.

Besides her taste and tact, her gaiety arrests your attention. Her whole personality is imbued with quickened, but controlled moods. She laughs with her eyes as well as her lips. This makes her presence vital. It is like a brilliant game. Actually, she need not do anything but simply be herself and straightway she fulfills her role—to entertain by enlightening. Her happy nature, guided by taste and tact, illuminates the humanly excellent which we seek and which delights us.

In the restaurant of a summer resort I once took a seat at a corner table where a feeble old man was sitting, waiting for his food. He told me that this was a good spot because you were usually served by a very nice waitress, a college girl. "You are right," I replied, "some waitresses are very anxious to serve you well, but usually only if you give them a good tip." "Not this young lady. She would wait on you graciously even without a tip. You have the feeling that she cannot be anything but pleasant to everyone," observed the old man. When I gave her my order I discovered in her that gay temperament that puts you at ease so that everything around you seems pleasant.

The American college girl embodies ennobling femininity. In her presence you definitely feel inspired to change your own life. You are gently impelled to see the beautiful and do what is good more simply, quietly and joyfully. Goethe's frequently quoted line: "The eternal feminine leads us on," is more easily understood in her presence. The agreeable thing about her is that she is not conscious of her fruitful influence, or scarcely so. Without intending to, she has an exhilarating effect. If she were self-conscious about it, she would forfeit her charm and with it her effectiveness. This unstudied, natural manner gives her feminine nobility the classic touch.

The American college girl represents a new aristocracy. We know about the aristocracy of blood, of money and of the mind. In the case of the college girl we may speak of the aristocracy of human cultivation. She is not born an aristocrat, she does not have much money, and her spiritual achievements are not world-renowned. But she is inwardly and outwardly cultivated, she has taste in her dress and tact in her behavior; she is friendly to human beings and conducts herself with dignity toward the world. This is the basis of her aristocracy. As an aristocrat of the purely human element she is a glowing part of her environment. The particular value of her aristocratic way of life lies in the fact that she is not impossible nor even a difficult model for the one who is prepared to follow her. Not everyone can belong to royalty, be a millionaire or create something of world significance. But everyone can make the moment more meaningful, give better form to each day, capture more joy for his own life and that of others. It is this which the aristocratic existence of the college girl stimulates us to do and invites us to emulate. And she will be neither hurt nor envious if you surpass her in the form you give your life. On the contrary, you thereby become interesting and admirable to her. She will seek your company and quietly respect you. She will take you as an example for herself and will call the attention of others to you. This is another characteristic of her nobility, which is not to be found among aristocrats of blood, money or of the spirit.

The college girl, moreover, proves to be an artist of life. Every artist struggles to give concrete form to an idea. He lets his idea live and speak, the poet through the word, the painter through his picture, the musician through tone. The idea of the college girl is humanitarianism, which she expresses in her cultivated personality. A dancer devotes herself passionately to the art of the dance. It is her goal to dance beautifully. The college girl devotes herself passionately to the art of human life. Her goal is to live in beauty and dignity. The one as well as the other is driven by an inner compulsion. Both must practice their art, which means hard work. Both strive for superior achievement in their field. However, whereas the creative artist struggles to conquer only one aspect of human life, the college girl tries to master all of human life. The difference is this: one serves a single, albeit particular part of the culture, whereas the other furthers the culture as a whole. But if it happens that a girl writes good poetry and is at the same time a good college girl, then she is twice an artist. She enriches poetry and life. She knows how to master the particular as well as the general. She serves the art of life and the life of art.

It is true, not every college girl is cultivated inwardly and outwardly in the same measure and to the same extent. The progress of her work at self-cultivation in college depends to some degree—some observers think, largely—on who her parents were, in what kind of home and neighborhood she grew up, what schools she previously attended. Her education and her self-cultivation in college are undoubtedly influenced by all these factors. A girl who comes from a good family, who has previously attended good schools and is by nature intelligent has, of course, a better chance to work her way up to higher levels of self-cultivation than one who comes from indigent circumstances and who is less capable of adjustment. But college offers the one as well as the other the best possibilities of development. In most cases the college tries to treat each one individually. The weaker one is given special consideration, so that she, too, can make the grade. As a rule, however, human beings are like plants. Even though they are grown in the same carefully prepared soil, nourished with the same food, they do not all thrive equally well, although the seed comes from the same stalk. The weaker ones, even if they are given special attention, do not often attain the magnificence of the stronger ones.

Students can be divided into three groups. The first group includes all those who wanted to go to college, who have the ability and who are supported by their parents. They feel at home on the campus. They are in the majority. The second group comprises those who have the desire to go to college and who are being helped by their family, but who do not have the necessary qualifications. Not every girl is capable of advanced study. To that group belong those who enrolled in this particular college only because their parents wished it. If they had had their choice, they would probably have decided on another school or would have done something altogether different. They are not quite at home on the campus. To the third group belong those who have the urge and the ability to study but who get little or no support from their parents or from other sources. They are at home on the campus, but they are usually tired. A girl in this category does not, of course, look the same as the fortunate one who can study without worries. But they all, in varying degrees, show the marks of the noble house in which the spirit and the body of the young girl are excellently cared for. Even the girl who is able to remain only one year is richer when she leaves than when she came.

For an accurate, overall picture of the college girl it is also important to differentiate between an American girl and a foreign girl, a resident student and a day student, a student in a girls' college and one in a coeducational college, and finally between a college girl and a girl who does not go to college. Such distinctions make it easier for us to understand the characteristics of the college girl as well as the various levels of her cultivation.

A girl who lives and studies on the campus of a girls' college (a resident student) seems to have a better chance of cultivating her personality. She has more possibilities of developing into a genuine college girl. As a resident student she has more time. This and other favorable conditions seem to make it easier for her to reach her goal.

She seems more apt to succeed in developing a cultivated soul in a cultivated body.[15] There is no loss of time in traveling back and forth to lectures. She goes from her room to the classroom in a few minutes. Whereas her fellow students who are not resident students are subject to various distractions at home, she devotes herself undisturbed and with composure to her lessons. She can comfortably and in a relaxed mood take part in the cultural activities on the campus. There are fewer opportunities for a resident student to go out and there is less temptation to spend time and energy on things which do not serve her welfare. She is spared unnecessary distractions, senseless excitement and waste of time, all of which often beset the non-resident student. A resident student lives a quiet life, devoted to study, a life that is planned and organized. She moves in an environment in which everything is aimed at the development of her feminine nobility. Accordingly, she appears composed, rested, concentrated.

It is different with the day student who does not live on the campus but is there only for lectures. She must ride back and forth from her home to the college in a bus or an automobile. As a rule both ways take one to two hours. While she is dashing through crowded streets in the early morning vexed by the fear of being late, the resident student is leisurely making her final preparations for her first class. After classes, while one girl is feverishly working her way home through traffic, the other is resting on her bed in her room. At home the day student's time is usually taken up with hundreds of details. It is not easy for her to devote herself in peace and composure to the cultivation of her inner and outer self. Physically and psychologically she vacillates between the affairs of home and those of her place of study. And she shows this in her appearance: always busy, rather restless, usually tired.

The American girl generally knows the advantages enjoyed by a resident student. That is why she usually tries to live on campus, but of course only if she can afford to and if there are no other obstacles. It sometimes happens that she prefers campus life even if her home is quite near the college. I once asked a resident student whose parents lived within easy walking distance from the college why she did not live at home. She said she liked it better this way; she learned more and also had more opportunity to take part in the campus social life, which she particularly enjoyed.

Not only for practical but also for psychological reasons the resident student of a girls' college seems to have the advantage over the day student. She lives apart from her family and friends, sheltered from the noisy ways of the world. She keeps herself aloof. "If you would count for something, make yourself scarce," is an old proverb. The importance she takes on away from home becomes evident if we examine more closely her relation to her parents and relatives. They write each other often. They miss one another. Each meeting is like the exchange of a blessed gift. The happiness derived from this is unknown to the day student, for she is at home every day.

There is another characteristic of the resident student which her seclusion on the campus brings out. She is, as a rule, more feminine than other girls. She grows up remote from the world's confusion and from men's pursuing eyes. She looks out from her small world toward the large world with a certain distance and at the same time with longing. She knows that her residence on the campus is only temporary and that one day she will lead her own independent life outside. At the core of her dreams and plans is usually a man whom she does not yet know or, if she does, whom she sees less frequently than does the day student.

This dreaming and planning in seclusion also leaves its impression on her appearance. If on weekends or during vacation she appears outside among people she is fresh, rested, enthusiastic, full of life and ideas. Thus she meets her boy friend and other people who are fascinated by her young and cultivated spirit. The writer found these views confirmed in a conversation with a number of Princeton students. They also thought that the resident students of girls' colleges were in general more feminine and fascinating than other female students.

It is also interesting to observe the subtle difference between native and foreign resident students. In almost every girls' college one now finds foreign students. On the campus they have the same duties and enjoy the same privileges as the American girls. They could be at home here, and yet they are not, not the way an American girl is. The thing that is taken for granted by the native raises problems for the foreigner. Therefore, in her insecurity, she is more cautious, more reflective. She will seldom try to set the fashion here. Rather, she prefers to observe her hostess and adjust to her. If she does not succeed, she is lonely.

Moreover, she must often fight homesickness, for her home is usually thousands of miles away. Even an American girl is now and then overcome by homesickness during the first few days and weeks after her arrival on the campus, and this can move her to tears. But her homesickness soon passes. The foreign student, however, in some cases needs special care. She is generously and lovingly helped by her fellow students and also by the campus administration. In time she begins to feel at home. Guest and hosts learn from one another. The foreign girl learns what is unfamiliar and new to her in the American way of life. The hostess learns from the foreign girl those customs and traditions which shape and direct human life outside her country. Merely by observing each other's conduct and by associating with one another they become enriched. Sometimes they become good friends and correspond for years after they have finished their studies.

The resident student of a girls' college is also to be distinguished from a coed. Both have the same course of study, but they carry it on in a different environment, which again is different if the coed is also a resident student. The one girl moves in a world in which she meets almost no men except her instructors. In the world of the other there are many young men. We are tempted to conclude from this fact that the one cultivates her femininity and devotes herself undisturbed to her studies,[16] whereas the other takes on masculine attitudes of mind and is often diverted from her work.

We can best see the difference between the two if we carefully compare the two personalities as manifested by their behavior. We then discover in the picture of the resident student shades and nuances which are, in general, not to be found in the picture of the coed. These are subtle characteristics, more easily felt than expressed. But they rest primarily on the same basis which we pointed

out when we spoke of the difference between the resident
student and the day student. It is the factor of being
aloof—toward the man, also—which makes the resident
student seem fresher, more enthusiastic and more warmly
responsive than a coed who is a stranger to the mystery
of distance and of longing.[17] A person who has an opportunity to observe objectively the students of Radcliffe
and those of Wellesley, who are farther removed from
the male world of Harvard, will probably share this
view."

It must, however, be emphasized that the above-mentioned classification was primarily the result of the total
impression produced by all students. We were anxious
to show the college girl in her environment, to reveal
the influences of this environment on her development and
to present her in this light. In doing so we have given a
picture of the majority of students. Individual cases will
contradict this picture. It is, of course, always possible
that some particular day student of a coeducational college who flirts with her boy friend between classes and
lets herself be taken home each day after classes may have
better grades than a day student who goes out perhaps
once a week with her boy friend. Nor do we deny the
possibility that a particular resident student of a coeducational college may have more feminine social charm than
a student on an all-girl campus.

The cultivated soul in the cultivated body—this image
of a human being is recognizable in every group of female
students, even though the individual features vary from
person to person, and the degree of cultivation differs.
The college girl, irrespective of the group to which she
belongs within her world, shows an objective and a sub-

jective cultivation which is usually denied the non-college girl.

A young American woman who does not attend college lacks these advantages: the development of her intellectual powers, the polish of her manners, better career possibilities and perhaps, also, the opportunity of making a better marriage. She lacks the higher level of cultivation which as a rule she obtains only in the cultivated and educative environment of the campus. For her, completion of high school means a farewell to formal education; for the college girl it means the beginning of higher education. The one has stood still, the other has gone ahead. During the time when the non-college girl sits at her typewriter in an office or sorts out quantities of hosiery in a department store, or sings lullabies to her newborn baby in a tiny apartment, the college girl is discussing exciting problems in the classroom, reading scientific books in the library or relaxing in witty conversation at a social gathering. The two young women move in different worlds which have scarcely anything in common. Slowly a chasm forms between them, even if they happen to have come from the same locality and attended the same high school.

In the waiting room of a small railroad station, a college girl once met a friend from high school who was not a college girl. Each had come there to meet relatives. I was struck, first of all, by the difference in their outward appearance. The one had neatly combed hair and well-groomed hands. The hair of the other was done up in curlers; her fingernails were chewed off and showed remnants of red nail polish. The one was carrying a book by Dante, the other had just been reading a *True Love* story.

In their conversation they did not talk the same language, for their fields of interest were miles apart. The college girl, for instance, said that she was looking forward to the symphony concert next Saturday, to which the other girl replied that this was not for her, she would go dancing somewhere over the week end. On one subject, however, their interests merged. That was baseball. They both spoke enthusiastically about it.

A Greek sage was once asked the difference between a cultivated and an uncultivated human being. "The cultivated one is alive, the uncultivated one, dead," replied the wise man. The difference between the college girl and the non-college girl does not seem to be so great, but it is great enough. A few of the more wide-awake girls later realize what they have missed by not attending college. Some try to make up for it by enrolling in college extension classes. Others decide to continue their education after their children have grown up and left home. There are also some who try to compensate for their loss by mere imitation of cultivated persons. In most cases, however, such education acquired in a roundabout way is only a substitute. They lack the natural luster of the cultivated soul in the cultivated body, which is characteristic of the college girl.[18] The image of femininity she presents is finer, richer, wiser and perhaps closer to the one we are longing for.

The Various Types

They all, just as they are, know how to use their time meaningfully and beautifully, each in her own way.

In the preceding chapter we described the college girl's appearance and the measure of her cultivation, which are primarily the result of her college environment. We shall now point to those features in the portrait of the college girl which are conditioned by her innate disposition and tendencies.

In one's association with female students one soon realizes that some are more concerned about intellectual accomplishments, others about social brilliance. I once observed three campus girls as they came upon an attractive little boy. One burst out spontaneously, "I'd like to have that one!" The other remarked, "Look at those big blue eyes—aren't they wonderful!" The third one pushed the boy's cap to one side so that it sat practically on his ear, which made him look like a ragamuffin, and remarked, "He looks nicer that way!" The first girl showed the maternal, the second the aesthetic, and the third the humorous aspect of her nature. Still others manifest romantic tendencies. There are also some whose main interest is in the field of religion, whereas some combine all these tendencies harmoniously in their personalities.

The Intellectual Type

The main goal of the student who is intellectually inclined is to excel in her studies. Her ambition is to do superlative work and get excellent grades. Her dearest friends are teachers and books; the rooms she frequents most are lecture halls and libraries. She is busy most of the time. One sees her browsing in reference books, looking up a particular article in the periodical room, waiting in the corridor for her instructor, or discussing a difficult problem with her classmate. The following factors usually have a decisive effect on her intellectual activity as well as on her success in her studies: her inner urge to tackle problems and to solve them; the stimulating awareness that in her class there is a Sylvia or a Margaret who is also ambitious and gifted and is also trying to lead the class; the admiration she gets for her good grades from her parents and friends. She feels pressure from within and without to develop her intellect, and she devotes herself to this with all her powers. The things which serve her intellectual progress little or hardly at all seem unimportant to her or of only incidental significance.

As soon as she wakes up in the morning she begins thinking about the problems that await her in lectures and texts. She cannot permit herself to go to class half prepared. She must know everything that is required— and more. She realizes that only a student who goes beyond her actual duties and adds something extraordinary deserves recognition. To get a superior grade she must master not only the material of her textbook and that offered by her instructor during class; she must read many more books and consult encyclopedias; in short, she must do additional research. For example, if French is her minor she is not satisfied merely to acquire a reading and speaking knowledge of French. She wants to know something about French philosophers, poets, statesmen and artists. She is also interested in the history of the country. Therefore she has little time for other things. In the morning while her fellow-students are still busy at their make-up or are chatting at the breakfast table, she is already hurrying to the library or is sitting alone in a quiet corner and once more going over the work she has prepared for her classes that day. She is a perfectionist. She must once more think through what she has just worked out, look at it from all angles, test it. Facts and hypotheses, proofs and conclusions, expressions and commas—everything must be absolutely perfect. Under no circumstance does she tolerate a solution which is only partly correct. She hates to hand in work that is half finished. A scientific problem which she has not yet solved troubles her in her sleep.

During class she usually sits in the front row. She wants to be able to see the teacher and the blackboard all the time. Not a spoken or written word must escape her. Nothing may elude her attentive eye. If something is being explained that she already knows, her thoughts skip ahead. For instance, if Plato's theory of ideas is being presented, she is already trying to find concrete examples to illustrate the problem, in order to submit them in the class discussion. If Napoleon's youth is being discussed, about which she has so often read in history books, she spends the time recalling the causes of his rise and fall. If it is a Latin class and the gerund is being explained, a form which is familiar to her, she will probably try to relate this form to others, to consider, for example, gerund and supine, in order to achieve clarity on a broader basis. Thanks to this effortless activity of her mind and her ambition to use her time profitably, she is always ahead. She has progressed to a level which others must still attain. She is often called "our big sister" by her fellow-students, and justifiably so.

In class it is usually "big sister" who asks the most questions and volunteers the most answers. She shines in class discussions and even notices the teacher's mistakes. In fact, she is the one who rouses the learning-teaching community, pupil and teacher, and spurs them on to progress. She is the moving spirit, *le feu sacré* in the class.

This type of student is, of course, very ambitious. She struggles obstinately not only for superior achievements, but also for recognition of these achievements. The mark "Good" which would make many others very happy, disappoints her. The day on which she gets a "B" is a dark day for her. Even when she gets "Very good" but discovers that another girl was given the same grade for a particular test, she is disturbed and curious to see that girl's work. She, of course, feels that her work is better, and she is amazed that she did not get "A+."

There was a case of a student who dropped a course in which she had been actively engaged for six months. The reason? She came to the conclusion that it would be impossible for her to get an "A" at the end of the school year. She did not want "B" along with "A's" in all her other courses. I know of another case in which a student dropped out of college at the end of her sophomore year and matriculated in another college with a high scholastic standing. She felt that the college she had been attending did not satisfy her intellectual needs and ambitions. Even though such cases are extreme and do not often occur, they are nevertheless characteristic of the ambitious striving of the girl who is intellectually gifted.

Other aspects of college life, such as social and athletic affairs or activities in academic societies, if they do not directly concern the progress of her studies, are given a secondary place in her program. Even the temptation to date is properly curbed. "No man can serve two masters," she thinks and goes to the telephone to tell her boy friend that she can go out with him only twice a month at the most. There is not much point in arguing about this; after all, she knows what she wants. "Study is more important to me than pleasure," she says determinedly. "If he is intelligent enough he will understand," she says to herself, and goes on with her work.

Her greatest pleasure is reading. It is her work and her passion. (She cannot visualize her future home without the built-in bookshelves.) If she gets tired of reading scientific books, she chooses books of literary value. Now and then, for relaxation, she may read detective stories or adventure stories. Occasionally she also goes to football games, takes time to attend jazz concerts and visits art exhibitions. Relaxation and variety—that is good, but not too much, nor too long, she thinks. It is necessary to be distracted in order to be able to concentrate better afterwards. She feels best in seclusion and concentration; it is then that she realizes her strength.

Once I attended a birthday party of one of my students. It was eleven o'clock when I was ready to go home. I was joined by a student who was going the same way. As we walked along she told me that she had come with a friend who wanted to stay longer at the party. She said she enjoyed the party but that her conscience bothered her because she would lose too much time if she stayed longer. Besides, she wanted to get a good night's sleep because she had an important test the following day. Among her fellow-students this girl had the reputation of being ambitiously intelligent.

The intellectual girl's heart belongs to her studies. She hopes to graduate *summa cum laude*. She is already making plans for her Master's degree and dreams about a Ph.D. The goal of her ambition is to win a Fulbright or a Woodrow Wilson Fellowship. Even though she has independent means for further study, the two award names have a potent effect on her intellectual striving. She knows that winning one of these fellowships would give her academic prestige; she would enter the intellectual elite.

I happen to know of the following case. An ambitious junior read in the paper that a female student of another college was granted a Woodrow Wilson Fellowship in the subject in which she herself was specializing. The girl took the weekend off, and traveled two hundred miles to congratulate the fellowship winner and to learn how she managed it. The significant thing about this incident is that she traveled on borrowed money and that on the particular weekend her class was having a large party.

It is not necessarily true that only the naturally gifted have intellectual ambitions. On the contrary, many so-called child prodigies often have other than intellectual interests. The intellectual type includes all those—even those moderately gifted—who, with love and enthusiasm, with zeal and determination, devote themselves primarily to the search for truth. It includes all those who best embody the meaning of the word *studere*. "I like it, it gives me pleasure," the intellectual girl answers if one asks her why she devotes herself so assiduously to her studies.

But it would be wrong to imagine that the intellectual student to whom we are referring resembles that freak of former times, the book worm with spectacles, stooped gait and pallid complexion, her mind lost in books. It is very seldom that the intellectual on the campus of a girls' college reminds one of this type. In many cases she is even elegant, impressive-looking and always well-groomed. The environment in which she lives and studies sees to it that, despite her devotion to mental work, she also cultivates her appearance, a problem which is of particular interest to the socially-conscious student.

The Social Type

To be surrounded with people, amuse herself, have parties and celebrations—that is the chief interest of the college girl with social gifts. She likes her studies, but she likes sociability better. Hence she limits herself to what is most essential in her studies. After all, she needs time to entertain her old friends, both male and female, and to make new friends, to regale her friends and acquaintances with her social charm. She often finds it tedious to sit in the library for a long time among her books, or to work for hours on an experiment in the laboratory.

But she does it because it is required of her. She performs her work properly and conscientiously, for she has a highly developed sense of values in everything she does. It goes against the grain of the social type to be untidy or careless. If one sees that she is naturally intelligent and points out to her that she could achieve much more in her studies, she excuses herself by saying that it is impossible for her to study more because of her social obligations. In one of my classes I had two students who always sat together. They were both intelligent, but one of them did not study as much as the other. Once I commented to the dilatory one on the success of her neighbor, adding that she herself could be just as good if not better. "But Sylvia doesn't care about social life; that takes up a lot of my time, but I enjoy it," she said candidly.

When a young instructor first appears on the campus and is introduced to the students personally, the intellectual girl usually asks him, "What is your field? Of course you have your doctorate?" The society girl will probably want to know whether this is the first time he has been in this part of the country and whether he already has some acquaintances or friends. She is primarily concerned about human relationships and does not want anyone to be alone. She thinks that you get to know yourself properly only if you are often with other people, that in constant social intercourse you make yourself and others happy. She meets you with frank, glowing eyes and smiles as though you were a dear, long-awaited guest. That is the way she greets everyone, man or woman, young or old, acquaintance or stranger. She gives herself wholeheartedly to everyone she meets. Sometimes it seems as though she had nothing else to do, as though it were her first and foremost task to entertain. The amazing thing is that she does this with obvious joy. It is her forte to be friendly toward people, just as being studious is the forte of her intellectual fellow-student. The latter seeks seclusion so that she can devote herself undisturbed to problems and ideas, whereas the other longs for social affairs at which she entertains and is entertained, especially by people who are close to her.

A student with a social sense seems irreplaceable in all social affairs and events. Thanks to her enthusiasm and her original ideas, even the most casual gathering becomes an event. She is the guiding spirit of all social activities that take place on the campus and outside. Since her organizing ability is known among her fellow-students, she is usually on committees for all kinds of events and celebrations. She usually plays the part assigned to her with originality and charm.

She has the best time when she is entertaining others. Her contentment grows in proportion to the contentment of others about her. She makes an effort to have everyone feel more at home than he does in his own home. She treats everyone in an individual way. She knows what a person lacks, what he would like to have. She reads it in his eyes. If you observe how graciously she offers you a cup of coffee, how intimately she lights her neighbor's cigarette, how gallantly and freely she moves from one person to another, you will inevitably conclude that she is an accomplished hostess who feels the pulse of the company as if it were her own.

It is a pleasure for her to be in company and to shine in it, just as it is a pleasure for the intellectual to busy herself with her studies and to be a success in them. While the intellectual girl never quite feels the happiness experienced by the born social type among friends in a luxurious hotel or on the terrace of a country club, with music and wine, neither is the social type capable of feeling the profound happiness which the other type experiences in quiet and seclusion, with her books and ideas.

At the end of a party many people say or think, "Thank God it's over!" or, "I'm glad I can go home again!" Others, however, say or think, "It was wonderful. Too bad it's time to break up!" The latter do not always belong to the social type, just as the former are not necessarily intellectual types. It depends on what the individual girl expects from a party.

Social grace is everything for the social type. She concentrates on it, and accordingly chooses the magazines and books which she reads in her spare time. It dictates the choice of her make-up and clothes. To this end she learns bridge and tennis, and she regrets that she cannot play the piano better or that her voice is not good enough so that she can sing. All this would add to the brilliance of her social success. She dreams of one day being chosen queen of the ball.

A student who has a talent for sociability will entertain you even if you do not entertain her. This is perhaps the most charming attribute of her personality. She really has a sixth sense for combating boredom and invoking an increased feeling for life. When she beckons with her hand or her eyes, when she smiles or says something to you, when she gently presses your arm or lightly grazes your shoulder in passing—all this takes place almost intuitively, tactfully, at the proper moment, in the right situation. It is in no sense familiar or intrusive. It is nothing more than a charming way of entertaining you. That is why she is admired and sought out. When she leaves, you wish she would return. You feel better when she is around. No one feels lonely or abandoned in her presence. Here one easily perceives the old catholic truth that to be in the company of a friendly human being is a delightful experience. (*"Nil homini amicum sine homine amico."* St. Augustine) She teaches a lesson in human sympathy that is needed to affirm life.

The intellectual student shines in class, the socially-minded student, outside of class. The student who shines both in and out of class is the aesthetic type.

The Aesthetic Type

What constitutes the brilliance of the aesthetic type? Her consciousness of beautiful form. She is interested primarily not in what one thinks, says or does. She puts the emphasis on *how;* that is to say, she is concerned about thinking, speaking and acting beautifully. Her chief requirement seems to be to develop and cultivate beautiful personality forms. She is an imaginatively gifted person, able to provoke aesthetic pleasure through her appearance, movement and words. The word "adorable" spoken by her is not just another high sounding adjective. It gives body and soul to love and admiration. As a result, her deep sense of appreciation becomes impressive. An M.I.T. graduate wrote to one of my students: "You have something which lifts me to a heaven of pure bliss." An object of beauty, an aesthete *par excellence,* she had the ability to awaken the sense of aesthetic experience of which she herself was immensely capable.

Her outward appearance, above all, reveals her aesthetic taste. In her make-up, in the color combination of her clothes, in her choice of jewelry, in the grooming of her hair and hands, in the way she is dressed—in all these details one discovers the care and order that bear witness to her unusual sense of beauty. The way she looks or laughs, the way she stands or walks, the way she grasps the situation—all combine to make her behavior like a beautiful poem.

The beautiful poem, however, is not a spontaneous creation. It requires talent and work. In the case of the aesthetic type, talent is expressed in her innate sense of beauty; work, in her cultivation of graceful form. This conditions the aesthetic image of her nature. What nature has given us we must make our own, even aesthetic taste. Thus she learns beautiful form from books, from works of art, from people and nature. She is always discovering something for herself—a sentence she reads, a line in a work of art, a tone in music, a gesture as she converses with another person, the harmony of colors in a blossoming garden. Minor objects and occurrences, disregarded by many, are perceived by her as treasures and stored away. With them she adorns the house of her personality.

While the intellectual girl is reading her report, perhaps for the fifth time to make sure there is not a comma missing, and while the socially-minded girl is busy decorating the hall for the next dance, the aesthetic girl is leafing through fashion journals, polishing her fingernails, sitting in front of her mirror to perfect a hair-do, or she is stretched out on the couch in her room, taking a beauty nap. Her scrupulous attention to her appearance means more to her than a pastime. It is necessary for her because it accentuates her personality. She has the gift of seeing the beautiful and the urge to realize it within herself. She spends whatever time she has in doing this. She must follow her destiny; that is, she must perceive beauty and let it shine forth. She cannot do otherwise.

If we observe the college girl who has a definite aesthetic tendency, both on the campus and outside, we realize that in comparison with others she is more original, neater, gentler and quieter, more distinguished. Her originality is expressed in her dress, her make-up, her entire behavior. In class she sits up straight; she would never allow herself to slouch or sit carelessly, or even perhaps rest her chin on her hand. What is original about sitting up straight, one might ask? The fact that it keeps one supple and does not give the least impression of stiffness, we might answer. She avoids handing in her written work with words crossed out, just as she would never set down a cup of coffee with some of the liquid spilled in the saucer. This shows her particular love of order which marks everything she does. Her soft step, her undemanding look, testify to the gentleness of her quiet, balanced spirit. She would never be insistent, come too close, impose herself, disturb one. If a teacher, for instance, announces an unexpected test, a few students will generally express their dissatisfaction. Not so the aesthetic girl; she may simply smile. It offends her to be loud. If she opens the door or the window she takes care to do it quietly. And she moves her chair, any chair, without a sound. If she happens to drop her pencil on the floor she says, politely, "Pardon me, please." Through her manners she expresses a state of beauty that you love for its own sake. You perceive delight when you see her; it is the sort of delight you experience when you look at a young swan unconsciously revealing its beauty.

The summer theater of a resort town one evening put on a gay comedy. When the performance was over and the audience had left, a few girls lingered at the exit, exchanging their impressions, laughing heartily as they did so. One of them turned around and saw a few people resting on benches beside the illuminated fountain. "Girls," she said to her friends, "let's not laugh so loudly, we are disturbing the peace." She was a sophomore in a women's college.

Immaculate appearance and sensitive tact distinguish the aesthetic girl. Without intending to set herself apart, she attracts attention wherever she goes.

The driving ambition of the intellectual or the social type is usually foreign to the aesthetic type. In her splendor she is as unambitious as the rose in its beauty. Such an attitude is attractive. She gladdens by her mere presence, just as a picture by Miro, a poem by Longfellow or an overture of Brahms can make one glad. If one meets her privately or in public, during class or at a party, one always encounters the phenomenon of unusual grace characteristic of the aesthetic girl. The beauty emanating from her is doubtless a gift. But it would languish if it were not properly fostered. Yet it flourishes, thanks to the favorable atmosphere of the college world and the personal effort of the girl.

If we examine the picture which the aesthetic girl paints in her imagination or in her dreams of the future we are particularly struck by one that illustrates her taste. It shows a large modern house in which she would some day like to live. The house nestles against a hillside and has a distant view of mountain ranges or the sea. It is perhaps near an art colony or a community rich in creative activity and a common, fostering care for the best things of life. It has a garden which is a place of beauty and repose, a reflection of nature that awakens a mood in the soul. Do we see children? Yes, they are clean and attractively dressed. They are not yelling like savages and pelting each other with stones. They are playing nicely. Their mother is playing with them creatively by trying to awaken in them an intellectual and spiritual curiosity so that they will never be lonely in life.

The Classic Type

The intellectual girl is primarily concerned with the *what*, the aesthetic girl with the *how*, and the girl interested in social forms with the mere *fact* of thinking, speaking and doing. The classic type seems capable of uniting all three aspects and giving them equal consideration. It is not conspicuously evident that she is chiefly interested in study, in social life or in things aesthetic. She does not seem to be particularly gifted in any of these fields. Instead, she has the capacity of finding them all equally valuable and of practicing them together. Her strength lies in the fact that she harmoniously acquires the human values—the intellectual, social and aesthetic—and gives them back again in the same way. On closer observation one does not find occasion to say she is an intellectual, or she is a society girl or she is aesthetic. But one sees immediately that she has something of all these types. The difference is that the characteristics which, for example, manifestly differentiate the intellectual from the aesthetic type are so organically combined in her that one cannot draw sharp boundaries, even though they are obviously present, if not pronounced.

For example, if one talks to her one realizes that she is well oriented in her field of study, that she shows an interest in conversation for its own sake, and that she has grace and charm. She has the gift of devoting herself to several fields at once without losing her balance. The acute sense of order in her daily routine is a strong point of her character. To do first what is necessary, second what is useful, and third what a pleasant, is for her a sensible thing. The intellectual world is exactly as important to her as success in society, and beauty concerns her no less. One of these may not be neglected at the expense of another. Her ideal is a college girl who studies well, finds her way about graciously in the social world, and whose appearance breathes grace and charm always and everywhere. She struggles toward the integration of her personality. Any excess, no matter how impressive, is foreign to her. In her striving for the better forms of human life she heeds the principle of moderation and balance. She works on herself as well as her environment in the spirit of *viae aureae*, to use an expression of Horace. This gives her personality its classic stamp.

In the following pages we shall describe a number of situations which will show, on the basis of comparison and delineation, the character of the types we have spoken of (including the classic type) in their manifold forms. By way of introduction we should say that names and situations have been invented to illustrate the types.

There is Dolores, the intellectual; Carol, the social type; Rita, the aesthetic; and Renate, the classic type. They are all juniors and are spending a weekend on the campus. It is Saturday. On Monday they all have important examinations to take. In the forenoon they are going to study in the library; in the evening they are attending a social event.

How do they begin their day?

When Dolores wakes up she quickly glances at her watch. "It is late, I must hurry," she says. Then she asks her roommate about a particular book that she could use in preparing for her examination. She washes herself hurriedly and puts on the first dress she finds when she opens her closet door. Without further ado she goes down to the cafeteria. On the way she is stopped by a freshman who excitedly tells her that she has just seen a mouse and that she is still terribly frightened. "Interesting," says Dolores and hurries on. In the dining hall she sits down at an empty table, eats a little and goes straight to the library.

When Carol wakes up she tells her roommate in detail that she dreamed about her friends. She hopes they will be present at the evening affair. She leisurely performs her morning toilet and for a long time she considers what dress to wear in the evening. She waits until her roommate is ready, then they both go down to breakfast. On the way they meet another student. Carol asks her whether she is going to the social event in the evening. In the dining hall she sits down at a table where most of the girls are seated. She likes to talk during a meal. Then she goes over to the reception room to smoke a cigarette and talk some more. She stays a half hour; then she, too, goes to the library.

The first thing Rita asks her roommate when she wakes up is, "Is the sun already shining?" She says that she always wants the sun to shine on Saturdays. She takes her time under the shower and again in front of her mirror with her make-up. Before she puts on her dress she goes to the window to see what the weather is like. The colors of her dress are always chosen to conform to the moods of nature. On the way to the cafeteria she joins a classmate. Rita tells her that she is looking forward to spring and summer so that she can get brown again in the sun. During the meal she sees her friend, an art student, at the other end of the dining room. She goes up to her and asks her whether the piece of sculpture she was working on is finished. After breakfast she takes an hour's walk on the campus.

"Another Saturday. I hope it will be a nice one," says Renate as she gets up. After she has bathed and dressed, she quickly glances into her closet to see whether the dress she plans to wear that evening should be ironed. She takes her class notes which she might need in the library, says "So long," to her roommate and leaves the room. On the stairs on her way to the dining hall she meets a friend who invites her to drive into town to shop. Renate thanks her. She would love to come along, she says, but today it is impossible. She has to prepare for her examination, and also help with preparations for the evening's event. At breakfast she sits down with her fellow-students, chats with them, admires the engagement ring of a student sitting opposite her, and then goes to the reception room to hear what's new. But she stays only about ten minutes. For another ten minutes she enjoys the early morning air on the campus and then goes to the library.

How do these girls behave in the library?

In the corridor a new book is exhibited in a prominent

place. It is a large volume on twentieth-century painting, with a strikingly impressive cover. It is set up on a table very near the entrance to the reading room. Dolores is so preoccupied and in such a hurry that she does not even notice the book. Carol sees it and walks over to look at it. At that moment, however, she is hailed by a fellow-student. They step to one side to talk. Then Carol goes to the reading room without paying any further attention to the book. Soon Rita comes along. She quickly steps up to the book, examines it with great interest, leafs through it, writes down the author's name and asks the librarian whether, later on, the book can be taken out. Renate, in passing, notices the book and wants to look at it but at that moment she, too, is interrupted by a student. After a brief conversation she returns to the table and examines the book. Then she also enters the reading room to prepare for the examination.

After two or three hours of intensive study they are all somewhat fatigued. How do they relax? Dolores discovers a classmate at the other end of the room who happens to be reading a periodical. Dolores knows that she is rather intelligent. She goes over to her to discuss a few technical questions with her. Carol, on the other hand, joins a few students who are going out for a cup of coffee and a cigarette. Rita goes to the periodical room to look through some illustrated magazines. Meanwhile Renate takes out a scientific periodical to read on Sunday. Then she, too, leaves the room and goes to the cafeteria for refreshments. On her way back to the library she meets a freshman who is wearing an unusual pullover. Renate takes a few minutes to admire the elegant garment on the girl.

What are their thoughts as they finish their preparations for the test? Dolores: "I hope I'll get an A+ again." Carol: "If only the questions aren't too difficult!" Rita: "Perhaps I'll manage a C." Renate: "I hope everything goes well."

All afternoon Dolores sits in her room and studies. Carol helps with the preparations for the evening affair. Rita spends most of the time in the swimming pool. Renate studies a bit, plays the piano, and finally helps Carol.

What is their attitude during the evening affair?

It is an academic gathering organized by the college literary society. The program consists of a lecture on European existentialism, to be given by a young instructor of a neighboring college. After the lecture there is to be a social hour with refreshments and light music. The audience consists of a number of students of the campus, a few instructors, as well as student-guests from neighboring colleges. Dolores, Rita, Carol and Renate sit together. Their first impressions of the speaker before the lecture: Rita, "He is good-looking; I'd like to meet him." Dolores, "I hope he has something worthwhile to say." Carol, "If he doesn't bring in a few jokes it will be boring." Renate, "He seems to be a smart young man." After the lecture: Rita, "His voice was marvelous." Dolores, "There were a few points he did not clarify sufficiently." Carol, "To judge from his presentation, I think the existentialists theorize to much." Renate, "I feel his material was well-organized and intelligently presented."

Then the informal or social part of the program begins. Rita moves over to the gramophone, Carol goes to the table of refreshments. Dolores waits for an opportunity to discuss the obscure points with the speaker. Renate hesitates a bit; her eyes are everywhere. She is ready to step in wherever it is necessary.

We must admit that the pure types we have just described would hardly be found among college girls or, for that matter, among human beings in general. It is quite possible that an intellectual girl has a highly developed aesthetic sense, or that an aesthetic type also has a superb social gift. It depends on where the chief emphasis of the native and the cultivated interest lies. In one person this may be easier to recognize than in another. In some cases it will be quite impossible to draw definite boundaries. Then we shall be justifiably inclined to regard the type as a mixture between the intellectual and the aesthetic, let us say, or to call the girl a classic type.

Moreover, it should be pointed out that these types can also convey different shades resulting from various temperamental aspects of the college girl. These may be called character accents.

In almost every large class a teacher will discover a few students who have the gift of humor. Their gift is so patent that it strikes everyone who meets them. This is the college girl with the temperament of a little imp. Her humor bursts forth spontaneously and unexpectedly. A mere word, a look, and everyone begins to laugh. The innocently naïve, the gently comical, but sometimes also the sparklingly witty appear in her. In no time at all she can create a mood of hilarity. Now and then her flashes of wit may border on the ironic.

In a class in which only four students were registered, one of them once forgot her textbook. The instructor gave her permission to fetch it. When she came back she also had some chocolate bonbons which she distributed to everyone, including the instructor. Four weeks later the same student again forgot her textbook. This time the instructor said no when she wanted to get it. Then one of her fellow-students said: "Please, Doctor, give Helen permission. She'll bring us bonbons again."

Once I overheard a conversation about the advantages and disadvantages of large and small automobiles. One student spoke enthusiastically about the small European passenger cars. She said they were economical, easy to park, and usually trim in shape. Another girl retorted that in a large American car you stood a better chance of escaping with your life in case of a serious accident. "Even then a small car is better," replied its champion. "If you're driving a big Cadillac or a Chrysler you will probably drag yourself around on earth, groaning and lamenting over your broken bones, whereas if you have a serious accident in a Volkswagen or a Renault, the chances are that in no time at all you will be gaily flying about in heaven with the angels."

The imp among the students is also more informally dressed, chiefly in sports clothes that are different. Her hair is cut short, sometimes by herself or by a roommate. She doesn't bother much about her make-up. Once in a while you may see her in torn sneakers. On the dance floor she excels not in the waltz but in the cha-cha. The beatniklike life also interests her from time to time.

There are those who actually themselves live like beatniks or outsiders or "outlaws." You may call this kind of college girl frustrated, desperate, angry and rebellious. She is a turbulent person, confused, dissatisfied with herself and the environment—a favourite target of current novelists, social scientists and clinical analysts. She has conflicts with her parents, is absent-minded in classes, and breaks dormitory regulations. She hates examinations and rules controlling her behavior. She wants to live her own adult life, without having any preparation for it. Many of her afternoons and evenings are wasted in idleness and hanging around on the campus or outside of it. Sometimes she is possessed by *Weltschmerz*, another time she gets so bored that she wishes something would happen to break the monotony; then again she has moments when she enjoys her intense yearning greatly. The scholastic "die and become" is strange to her; the process of her refinement seems to be slow. She is usually the one who drops out of college or holds out in it with considerable difficulties. Tensions and conflicts exhibited by her often reflect the characteristics of those who appear to be well-adjusted and smoothly balanced students. Once a student of mine remarked, "I feel quite often just like Salinger's Franny." She was a mixture of the aesthetic and classic type. The difference between the turbulent and, for instance, the classic one (or any other type described here) is that the former spends her time without any urgency and control, while the latter uses it with determination and discipline.

The college girl with a maternal nature is different. There is usually nothing striking or extraordinary about her. She is always open-hearted, conscientious and dignified, like a person who knows what she wants. What is it that she wants? To complete her college work successfully, marry and have a family. This definitely fixed goal determines her conduct on the campus and outside. While others contemplate further study, or the advantages of a professional career, or do not know what they want, and are concerned about how to spend their time usefully and pleasantly in this small world and later on in the larger one, she is concerned about conscientiously fulfilling her duties on the campus, and she cheerfully accepts everything that is offered her. At the same time she is quietly thinking about how, later on, she can best serve her husband as helpmate and her children as mother.

During an informal meeting arranged by natural science students, I once had a conversation with a senior in connection with a paper on Wernher Von Braun. I asked her what she expected to do after graduation. She replied point-blank that she would marry and have a family. She said that if she could have had her wish, she would have married right after high school. But her parents had persuaded her to go to college first, and she was now convinced that with a college education she would be more valuable to her husband and children. "The mother of Wernher Von Braun must have been a wise woman," she added, "to buy her boy a toy telescope instead of a gun."

When this type of girl goes out with her boy friend she does not merely want to have a good time with him; she also wants to test him to see whether he is capable of being her companion for life and the father of her children.

Different from this type is the college girl with an erotic nature. She is interested above all in amusing herself. She does not think of marriage as yet. She rarely has the wish to have a family of her own. "There's plenty of time for that," she says. "First I'd like to be free to enjoy life." Where does she enjoy life? On the dance floor, on the sports field, in the theater, at cocktail parties —always accompanied by one or more admirers. She feels perfectly at home in an open sports car, sitting beside an athlete. In this sort of life lies her strength, but also her weakness. She may be a success with her admirers, but she is a problem for her parents and the campus administration. She may be excellent in dancing and flirting, which she loves, but she is only fair in studying and in being orderly, for which she has no time. Love letters and telephone calls keep her from studying. The fact that she cuts classes too often and repeatedly comes home late from dating brings her into conflict with the campus authority. Usually, however, the administration's wise handling of the situation and the example of her steadier and more self-controlled fellow-students with whom she is in daily contact help her to curb her erotic urges. She is made to realize that it is wiser to partake of the fullness of life in moderation than to enjoy only a part of it to excess.

The college girl with religious tendencies has other interests. If a religious problem is raised during class it is she who asks questions. When others take out a book on art or literature for the weekend, she selects one of a religious nature. She also takes part more often in religious gatherings than her fellow-students. During vacation she helps the minister in Sunday school, sings in the church choir, and visits the sick of the neighborhood. If she is of the Jewish faith, she wants to marry a rabbi; if she is Protestant, she would like to serve God and man as the wife of a clergyman; if she is Catholic, she often wonders whether it would not be better to become a nun.

We also come across the college girl with an evenly balanced nature. In her we do not recognize any of the above-mentioned character traits in particular. They are organically combined and manifested in a certain equilibrium. Structurally this type corresponds to the classic type.

We scarcely find unmixed character accents, just as we discover no really pure types. One girl can be impish and at the same time erotic; in another we detect religious as well as maternal symptoms, even though in different measure. Nor is it exceptional for one person to have equally strong religious and erotic tendencies.

If you were to meet a group of college girls whom you know very well, either after class on the steps of the lecture building or after lunch over a cup of coffee in the cafeteria, you could, if necessary, say offhand, "This is Lucia, an aesthetic type with character accents of a balanced nature; this is Jane, a mixture of the intellectual and social type with maternal character accents; this is Ann, the classic type with religious accents; and this is Sally, the social type with impish and erotic character accents." They all, just as they are, know how to use their time meaningfully and beautifully, each in her own way.

The American college girl teaches you quite often the Chinese precept that "It is better to light a single candle than to curse the darkness." That occurs without her planning to do so. It happens because of her spontaneous wish to make the room bright, to have the air fresh.

After World War II many American student groups went to Europe to help in reconstruction. Among them there were also college girls. They were neatly and simply dressed. To help those in distress they had packages of food and clothing sent from home; they made soup, not only for their countrymen, but also for the hungry children of refugees and for people whose homes had been destroyed by bombs; they distributed chocolate and toys among the children. They were friendly, helpful and kind to everyone they met. In their faces and in their movements one could see a childlike quality. A young Belgian student who had an opportunity to observe one such group more closely remarked, "Now I believe that America has a culture."

The Architect of American Culture

She creates the life of joy which her grand-parents dreamed of, her parents contemplated, and which she herself is now living and will hand on to her own children.

The people who discovered America, who built it up and made it great, were refugees.

Even Christopher Columbus can be thought of as a refugee. In his odes, the poet, Paul Claudel, points out that Columbus, on his dangerous ocean voyages, did not intend to discover a new continent. But tormented by a great spiritual unrest, he left his native land and sailed out to sea to the vast unknown, in order to calm himself and find a home for his searching soul.[19]

The emigrants who later flocked to this country from all corners of the earth were to a large extent also spiritual refugees. Some sought asylum here for religious or political reasons, some were driven to this hemisphere by their love of adventure or their fear of just or unjust punishment. Even the man who left his native land to escape poverty and create a better life for himself in the

150

new world will agree that it was not wholly the desire for material gains which attracted him to the U.S.A.

Thus they all came here to forget their unrest, and in the hope of having their dreams come true. Most of them were not disappointed. They were permitted to worship God as they wished without being persecuted, to discuss political questions openly and without fear. They found great opportunities for their talents and ambitions. No one cared how they had lived before. They earned their daily bread and discussed world trends in comfort and security. Gradually, in their daily struggle to make a better living, they forgot their inner unrest. Finally they felt at home here.

Then they turned their attention to their children. In order to protect their children from the anguish of spiritual homelessness which they themselves had endured, to a greater or lesser degree, they were determined to create a home in which their children would be happy and from which they would never have to flee.

This noble endeavor was and is today accomplished in growing measure by virtue of democratic training and education.

In the United States unusual interest is shown in education and training. Nowhere else in the world do people talk and write about it as much as here. No other country has so many schools, libraries and laboratories. Here there are hundreds of foundations and societies organized to promote science and art. Day by day there is a passionate search for new ideas. New methods are constantly being discovered and tested. Training and education in the democratic sense are the credo of the entire nation. Americans are convinced that only a trained and educated person who knows how to run his life successfully is really at home here, and that the more training and education one has, the more one gets out of life. This is also the point of view which governs higher education for women.

In the United States, college is the place where a girl finds her spiritual home. She comes here to acquire more knowledge, develop better taste and learn to understand herself and others better. The dream of her ancestors and the wise hopes of her parents have become personified in her, for she—the college girl—seems to be truly at home in the United States. And everyone who is perfectly at home is happy.

What kind of happiness does she experience in college, her spiritual home? From her first day of college to her last she experiences the happiness of intellectual, social and aesthetic growth. We have constantly pointed this out in the preceding discussion. Now we have come to the question: What is the meaning of her college education in terms of happiness? Later on she will directly or indirectly educate in terms of happiness all those who are entrusted to her care and with whom she comes in contact.

At the end of her college training she will either do graduate work toward a higher degree, take a position, or get married. The majority of girls marry, of course, though not always immediately. In order to find out what the college girl expects to give her children later on, or her pupils if she becomes a teacher, I asked several students in various departments, on the last weekend of the semester, to put down some of their ideas on the subject.

In the following pages I present a selection of these comments.

A student of education writes:

During my study I have gradually come to the conclusion that in order to be successful in life it is not enough to have talent. You must also work hard. So I shall see to it that my children study and work hard. But I, myself, shall care for their physical and spiritual welfare just like the tiny wren mother who, according to a report by Professor Arthur A. Allen, flies back and forth 1214 times a day from sunrise to sunset bringing her fledglings morsels of food. One of our instructors once told us the following story: A poor family had six children. All of them attended college and graduated with honors. When the mother was asked how that was possible, she replied that she had always seen to it that, from the first day of school, her children sat in the front row. I find that very good. I shall do the same with my children later on. I know from myself that it is much easier to be attentive if one sits near the teacher. I shall insist that, from the very beginning, my children prepare each lesson well. I know that I would have had a much better grade in Latin if I had not been inattentive during the first class lessons.

In a discussion of modern methods of education our professor once told us the following incident: He once met an old man who came from the slums of Brooklyn. He was an immigrant and spoke broken English. He said that he had three sons. One of them was a physician, the second an engineer and the third a Protestant minister. The professor wanted to know what method he had used in bringing up his sons. "None," replied the old man, "but in my spare time, when my boys were still going to school, I would often walk through the streets with them. If we met a man who was shabbily dressed, unkempt and un-shaved, perhaps also intoxicated, and who reached out his hand to beg for a nickel or a cigarette, my boys would ask, 'Father, why is he so poor and unhappy?' I answered, 'Instead of going to school he roamed the streets and did not obey his parents; today he is paying for it.' And when they saw a well-groomed, well-dressed man step out of a new car, the boys wondered, 'Father, he must have lots of money. Who is he?' 'He is a physician or an engineer,' I always replied. 'When he was a small boy he did not spend all his time on the playground, he obeyed his mother and was always at the head of his class. That is why he is a rich gentleman today.' This worked wonders with my sons," the old man remarked after a thoughtful pause.

I shall never forget what this professor told us about the old man. It taught me the effect of a positive and a negative example. That is the way I shall try to influence my children.

I learned another thing during my study. In order to be really successful you have to do more than your duty. No one talks about a soldier who does only his duty; he will never be promoted. It is only if he does something extraor-dinary that he is honored and given a citation. Our dean pointed this out to us last year in his address to the grad-uates. I shall tell my children about this soldier.

A sociology student wrote the following:

I have learned a great deal from my sociology books, not only for my examinations, but also for life. The works of famous sociologists help me to understand the structure

of our society. But the informal discussions we have once
a week help me particularly. Here each of us can propose
a theoretical problem or one taken from practical life for
general consideration. One of the students once told about
her grandmother and her aunt.

The husband of her grandmother died young and left
her a widow with seven children. She was very poor. But
always when she took her children's shoes to the shoemaker
for repair she gave the shoemaker's little son a nickel. This
boy later became a doctor and established a practice in his
home town. When her grandmother goes to him for treat-
ment and asks for a bill, he always says to her, "There is
no charge. When I was a small boy and poor you always
gave me a nickel." Even her grandmother's children pay
only half. Once her eldest daughter was a patient of his
and tried to pay him the full amount. "No," protested the
doctor, "I can only charge you half because your mother
is such a good woman and brought so much joy into my
poverty-stricken childhood." Later this daughter married
a well-to-do business man in New York. After a few years
she inherited ten thousand dollars from a neighbor who
stated in her will that she was leaving the money to her
because the daughter had always found time to make a
cup of coffee for her lonely and ailing neighbor and pass
the time of day with her.

These incidents from the lives of the grandmother and
aunt of my classmate disprove the old proverb that the
world repays you with ingratitude. I shall teach this to
my students and try to educate them to be grateful and
helpful.

I shall also make them learn by heart Longfellow's poem
about Florence Nightingale, which says that the suffering

turned to the wall to kiss her shadow when she passed their beds.

A student of natural science writes:

The last few years of my study have shown me more and more that life makes one famous and happy only if one serves truth and loves beauty. When we tire of always championing the truth, we turn our eyes to what is beautiful and thus refresh ourselves. This is my simple philosophy of life, which I hope to pass on to my students and my children.

I shall hold up to them Galileo and Thomas More as the heroes of truth. *"Eppur si muove"* ("But it *does* move") —that is what I shall impress upon my children as their motto for the courageous avowal of truth, which Galileo staunchly adhered to, in spite of threats and persecution on the part of his fellowmen. They shall also learn that Thomas More maintained his serenity even before the executioner, because he died for what he held true and sacred. These are supposed to have been his last words, addressed to the hangman, "When you cut off my head, please leave my beard intact. It did not commit any crime."

Since I am a passionate stamp collector, I shall also teach my students this interesting and instructive hobby. When I was still in grammar school I loved to remove the stamps carefully from envelopes, arrange them and paste them into my stamp album. I was always proud when I had a stamp that my friends did not have. In high school I was particularly interested in the different colors of the stamps. Today, in college, I discover that there is more to them. I am gradually realizing that, unconsciously rather than consciously, they symbolize the spirit and character of a nation. The star and crescent on the stamps of most Islamic peoples point to their tendency toward unreality. Hammer and sickle on the stamps of the Soviet Union appear as the instruments of slavery and despotism. The Statue of Liberty on the stamps of the United States holds her torch aloft for democracy and freedom.

In my children's room I shall hang a picture in natural colors of that wonderful bird (*passerina civis*) whose popular name is nonpareil, "having no equal." Its colors are truly incomparable; it looks as though it had been painted with a brush that was dipped in the rainbow. To me this bird is the symbol of all natural beauty. Its habitat is Florida, in the Miami region. I shall take my children there to show them this bird in its natural state.

A domestic science student writes:

On the campus I learned order and sociability, virtues which have changed my life.

At home I was spoiled and quite careless with my things. I often left my books and clothes lying around. I almost never made my own bed. My mother always patiently picked up and straightened things out for me. I did not have to help with the shopping or dishwashing. Instead my older brother or my father usually helped. My parents and brothers and sisters were very proud of me because I did well in school. I was always at the head of my class, and almost every other month my picture appeared in the local paper in connection with special school activities. That was probably the reason, or so it seems to me today, why I was given so much freedom at home. For the same reason I was also rather arrogant and haughty in my association with people, even in my attitude toward my school-mates.

On the campus I learned to make my bed neatly every morning and tidy up my room. Here I met students who were just as intelligent as I or much more so. Thus I soon got over any feeling of conceit. In my daily life with others I also learned to understand and appreciate them, always to be considerate toward other people.

During vacation I now help my family with the house-work. At the same time I try to put into practice the theo-ries about household management which I have learned in class. My family enjoys it and I feel that they also profit by it. Recently my older brother, who never had much use for me, said, "I wish I could marry a girl like my sister."

After graduation when I start to work, I will save money for a trip to Africa because I am eager to see how the people work and live there, and how the young lions play in freedom there. I believe in education through trav-eling.

A psychology student writes:

A few days ago I finished a paper on the behavior of old people. It was a rewarding subject for me. Now I know why some people are contented in their old age, whereas others spend their days in sorrow and bitterness. I also learned what an old person can mean to a young one and vice versa.

At the suggestion of my professor, I gathered the mate-rial for my paper in real life. Thus, during my summer vacation, I discovered an old couple in our neighborhood. Both of them were over seventy. He had set up a workshop in his garage where he built bird houses and feeding stations for the birds. Then he would give them away or sell them. She was busy in her garden during the summer, with her flowers and vegetables; in the winter she knitted and sewed for her grandchildren. Both looked happy and content.

Then I visited an old soldier, who had been an officer in the First World War. He is now over eighty. On his bookshelves I counted thirty-four biographies of generals and leaders of various nations. "In them I study the virtues and vices of heroes," remarked the old gentleman. In the fifteen minutes of our conversation I learned more than if I had read books all day.

After that a friend introduced me to an old, unmarried woman who was retired but who worked without pay in the hospital for the Red Cross. I have seldom met such warmth and friendliness in a human being as in this old lady with the saintly face.

I observed other types, too, among old people. I saw some who hang about street corners for hours at a time. Others I heard complaining constantly about the fact that they had become old and useless and nobody wanted them. At that time I also read in our local paper about the suicide of a former businessman. In his farewell letter he said, "I am lonely, old and sick. I have no more desire to live."

While I was working on my paper, I thought a great deal about how to make the burden of age more bearable. I believe one should prepare a person through wise education while he is still young for a productive and cheerful old age, by arousing in him such love for life, for work or for an idea that he will never lose it, even under the most difficult circumstances. But we must also give old people a feeling that they are important to us. We must talk to an old, sick person the way Hemingway lets the boy talk to the old fisherman, in *The Old Man and the Sea:* "You must get well soon, for there are many things I must still learn from you, and you can teach me everything."

What I learned in this way has contributed to my understanding of human nature. The old person is not a burden, but a human being whom we need. We can make him very happy and learn a great deal from him. With this attitude I hope my students and my children will approach old people.

P. S. When I discussed the problem of old age with my roommate, she advised me to read Cicero's *De Senectute,* which I shall do.

A student of musicology:

I am in love with Wolfgang Amadeus Mozart. His music makes the world ten times more beautiful for me. I like all good music—even jazz I enjoy very much—but there is nothing like the melodies of Mozart. To me they are like the music of the angels, they are so simple and gay. In his sonatas, symphonies or operas, in every piece of music he wrote, we feel a spirit that carries us heavenward. At least, that is the way I feel. The more you let yourself be permeated by his music, the more it frees you from everything that hurts or oppresses. You are put into a state in which you can only be happy. When I hear his music I should like to embrace everything—people and objects—out of pure joy. Then I feel as though I were riding straight to heaven in an elegant car. I am planning some day to write a book about Mozart, the child prodigy. I know there are a great many books about him. But mine will be different.

I shall illustrate it myself. I have already made a few sketches. My friends think they are wonderful. But I am not satisfied with them yet. It is all going to be much more beautiful, so beautiful that the boy Mozart will one day become the best friend of my pupils and my children, and replace in their minds the characters in their comic books. I shall explain to them the statement of my dear music teacher: "If you love Mozart, you will never be sad," and impress this upon them as their motto for life.

When I have saved enough money, my first trip to the old world will be to Salzburg. There I shall attend the Mozart Festival and become acquainted with the birthplace of my favorite composer. It is supposed to be one of the most beautiful places in the world. This trip will, of course, also furnish material for my book about the young Mozart, which I plan to write for the enjoyment of my children.

A student of literature writes:

My studies have given me a taste for the carefully chosen and polished word. You discover yourself in it and are made aware by it. You know who you are and vaguely realize who you ought to be. The revealing word of great writers and poets also teaches us to understand the course of world history, the mysteries of the human soul and of nature. So I shall influence my pupils to love the beautiful-sounding and meaningful word.

I shall explain to them sentences like the following:

From Shakespeare's *Timon of Athens:*

> Well, more gold;—what then?—
> Believe't, that we'll do anything for gold.

From Goethe's *Faust:*

> To gold still tends,
> On gold depends
> All, yes All. Alas, we poor.

From Saint-Exupéry's Le Petit Prince:

> Men no longer have time to understand any-
> thing. They buy things ready-made in shops.
> But there is no shop anywhere where one can
> buy friendship, and so men do not have friends
> any more. If you want a friend, tame me . . .

From Rilke's *Das Buch der Bilder:*

> We all are falling. This hand falls.
> And look at others: it is in them all.
> And yet there is One who holds this falling
> endlessly gently in his hands.

If my pupils or my children should say that they do not
quite understand lines such as these, I shall reply to them
in words similar to those of our professor of Spanish Literature. We were talking about Cervantes. Toward the end
of the hour the professor said that Tolstoy had read *Don
Quixote* three times in his life. When he read it as a young
man he is said to have laughed. The second time he read
it he was considerably older and he is supposed to have
been serious. When he read it the third time, he wept. I
raised my hand and said that I did not quite understand
the connection. "Tomorrow you will understand it better,
and thirty years from now it will be as clear as crystal to

you," replied the professor as the bell rang to announce the end of the class.

A student of history:

I was born and raised in a family of puritanical traditions. However, we are not as strict as we were when my mother was young. She said, for instance, that she was forbidden to read novels and that she was not permitted to make friends with a young man of another faith. Even now, although I am nineteen years old, I may not go out with a young man unless I have first introduced him to my parents. I am not allowed to smoke a cigarette or drink a Martini. When grandmother comes to visit us I may not appear in shorts. I may use lipstick only on special occasions.

I have a girl friend whose family are Quakers. She has been just as strictly brought up. On the campus I met and became friendly with girls who were brought up in other customs and traditions. I saw that they were freer and less restricted in their behavior. "What's wrong with smoking a cigarette or drinking a glass of wine in company?" a fellow-student once said to me. At first I thought this was strange. Now I see that it is harmless. On the contrary, it makes you more frank and entertaining, without offending good manners.

At my grandmother's deathbed my uncle had to promise that he would never marry a Catholic girl. But sure enough, he did marry a Catholic. This made him the black sheep of the whole family. Among my fellow-students, all of whom have different religions and ways of thinking, I have met many intelligent and valuable human beings who mean a great deal to me. Thus I have become more tolerant, not only toward others, but also toward myself. Recently I have become very much interested in Asian philosophy, especially Buddhism. I find that we can learn a great deal from the thinking of Eastern peoples, without giving up our Christian ideals. For the sake of wisdom my children shall read the philosophy of Zen, but for the sake of salvation they shall study the Gospels of Christ. I shall also influence my students along these lines.

An art student:

I should like to become a drawing teacher. I love to draw and paint. My mother tells me that even as a small girl I showed great interest in it. I prefer to paint landscapes. But I do not believe that I shall ever become a great painter. My teachers feel that I lack outstanding creative power, the feeling for the finer facets of objects. Perhaps I shall attain this. If I do not succeed, I hope that my pupils or my children will. I secretly hope that later on one of my children will be more successful in drawing and painting than I am, and live the life of Art.

In my home town I often help in a kindergarten during my summer vacation. "Draw a rabbit for me," one of the children will say. "Paint me a house," another will say. "Draw me a rocket," a little boy will demand. So we draw together many rabbits, houses, rockets and all kinds of other things. I am glad to make them happy. Some day I shall make my own children happy in this way, too.

My hobby is photography. With my camera I try to capture the subtleties which often elude my pencil and brush. I am interested in details which most people overlook about people and things in nature. Often in a snapshot I succeed in catching the impish laughter of a child. In other instances I take great pains over such interesting things as, for example, a limp sheet of newspaper on the street, a half-ripe tomato on a tray in a vegetable store, a buzzing fly in an empty room. I shall try to make my pupils and my children understand that in many cases the art of photography is like the art of poetry, for an unusual photograph is like an unusual poem.

I will show my youngsters the photographs that I took during my last trip to Europe. They will see clean, cultivated streets with well-kept houses in Copenhagen and Düsseldorf, they will notice the neat orderly villages with immaculate homes in Holland. These pictures should awaken in one of them a desire to become an architect who will design new American main streets which are neat and clean and attractive, and who will create new American suburbs which are not uniform, not flat, and not monotonous.

These statements are blueprints of the house of culture which the college girl is planning for herself as a person, for her students as a teacher and for her children as a mother. They give a glimpse of her knowledge and imagination, especially of the imagination that, on the whole, is more important than knowledge. In fact, imagination is needed to see facts. (The dreams of today's girls may become the actions of tomorrow's men. And with the same breath we repeat, if you educate a boy, you educate an individual, but if you educate a girl, you educate generations.)

The house of culture which the college girl plans and will build seems to be solid, comfortable and beautiful. How could it be otherwise? For it will be built by an architect who knows the importance of a firm foundation in everything, who is equipped with constructive will power and whose fine taste has been nurtured by the best education.

Besides talent and training, however, every architect who wishes to build a house needs the necessary means. America's technical success and her democratic system of education are the means at the disposal of the college girl. With these she creates the life of joy which her grandparents dreamed, her parents contemplated, and which she herself is now living and will hand on to her children.

In the material which the college girl will use to build the house of American culture, other nations may recognize traces of their own culture. Everyone, no matter on what continent he lives or to what people or religion he belongs, will find something in it that is familiar to him from his own home, along with much that he has never seen before.

In a campus theater of a women's college the foreign students once performed native folk dances. The costumes and dances of each group were different. The Brazilian dance was one of commanding passion; the French, delicate control; the Russian, vigorous footwork; the Hindu, lyrical movements of the hands; the Spanish, poised gaiety; the Japanese, chaste bowing. The American girl was the last to appear on the stage. She was not colorfully dressed. Her "national" costume consisted of a short, dark flannel skirt and a light-colored wool pullover. In her short hair was a little bow representing the American flag. She danced barefoot. In her graceful dance she combined all the finest expressions of her foreign fellow-students.

American culture as it is furthered by the influence of the college girl unites noble and pure culture elements of many nations. The American college girl adopts, molds and makes her own the spiritual achievements of peoples of all ages and hemispheres. These achievements become the components of American culture. There is no foreign culture in the United States; rather, it is a culture of the non-united states of the world. Its style is determined by American tradition and history and by the ideals and ways of life of the New World. Its flowering we see in the American college girl.

She is unacquainted with the feeling of homelessness that tormented her forefathers. Her contented life that seeks more substantial forms within a discontented and unfinished society represents the fulfillment of the aspirations of those immigrants who came to the New World in order to be ultimately and truly at home here. Thus her life is the model dwelling of American culture whose goal is increased happiness in the world. And wherever there is happiness, the feeling of homelessness disappears. Hence, the racial problems in her own country are to her of great concern, and she thinks that what Sir John Slessor suggests is both clever and wise, "People who live in glass houses should not throw 'little rocks.'"

If we look at a beautiful new model home we are tempted to own it. If we are familiar with the gay, simple life of the college girl we are inclined to share it in our own way. We are attracted to it and at the same time instructed by it. It manifests the growth of the distinctive American culure. This should be pointed out to anyone who for any reason is prejudiced or skeptical about present-day American culture. Faced with the image of the college girl, he will forget the selfish dealings of Wall Street, the criminal deeds of Chicago gangsters, the moral corruption of Hollywood, and the political scandals of Washington. The future of the United States will seem promising to him.

"I quit smoking and chewing gum and I don't touch cocktails anymore. I would like to be selected for the Peace Corps." This was spoken by a junior of a women's college to an acquaintance during a private party. When I heard this, I asked myself, "Is she one of the pioneers of the changed America?"[20] Her pledge reveals, in fact, the spirit of initiative that might change the image of the American Spirit.

To substantiate this we may mention one of her characteristics, namely, her lack of envy. She admires the success of her fellow-students with sisterly affection in work, parties and dating. Jealousy and envy as it is often found in the semi-cultured world are usually foreign to her. Thus she sets an example for the embodiment of pure culture in human association.

It was a rainy and gloomy late spring day; it was also the time of the final examinations on the campus. I went from the library down to the lunchroom to get a cup of coffee. On the way in the rain I met one of my students; she was glowing with joy. "You look in high spirits today," I said. "Yes, Doctor, I am very happy . . . Barbara got B in Logic . . . She failed the course last term. I tutored her and she did well on the last exam. She is happy, her parents are happy, I am happy, and her teacher, I suppose, is happy, too. Oh, I am so excited."

Conclusion

*She has learned how to take care of herself
and how to help others.*

"Not everything is as rosy as it has been described
here," said a teacher who had spent many years in a girls'
college, after she read the preceding account. "Many girls
are spoiled in their way of life, they are superficial in their
studies, hypersensitive in their association with others, and
want to have too much of a good time."

This is true of some college girls and these negative
characteristics are not accidental. They have their origin
in American civilization. For, in spite of her cultivation
and her uniqueness, the college girl remains the child of
American civilization. This civilization, despite its material
advance, must still accomplish a great deal in the spiritual
realm in order to attain the "perfection of man" which,
as Adams said to Jefferson, is the goal of the American
republic.[21]

But as for the college girl, we must add that even
though she is spoiled, she is not demanding. If one points
out to her that something must be done more thoroughly,

she gladly does it over. If one approaches her with understanding, she easily controls her oversensitiveness. Her
possibilities of pleasure-seeking are limited by her academic dignity which the campus spirit influences her to
uphold. This means that her weaknesses are less, thanks to
her college training, than those of her contemporaries who
have had no higher education.

Another colleague, after reading this essay, wrote: "The
portrait of the American college girl that you have tried
to draw seems to be generally bright. Did you really find
no dark shadows in your model? Or did you purposely
wish to show the splendor of the human being, using the
college girl as your medium, in contrast to the misery of
man which you movingly portrayed in your study of the
refugee?"

The weaknesses of which we spoke earlier may be regarded as the dark shadows in the bright portrait. Actually, they are not so dark as to obscure the beauty and
value of the picture. They are, rather, small imperfections
which point to the inadequacy of human nature in general
and the character of American civilization in particular.
Many people do not see these imperfections; some regard
them as natural or human, and only the demanding are
disturbed by them. We are reminded of cut diamonds.
Absolutely pure diamonds scarcely exist. Usually they
contain small specks of carbon which many people do not
see, while some even value the flaws as evidence of the genuineness of the gems. Only a few are disturbed by them and
seek absolute perfection which, in sober fact, they seek in
vain.

It is true, the life of the refugee is as different from that
of the American college girl as night is from day. Coming

from refugee camps in Germany to the campus of a girls'
college in the U.S.A., I felt as though I had stepped from
the world of suffering into the world of joy. This contrast
made a deep impression upon me. So I decided to paint
the other, the bright side of human life.

A future historian discussing the twentieth-century de-
cline of European culture will probably illustrate his discussion with the picture of the refugee. He will undoubtedly remark: "The short-sighted policy of the United
States was partly to blame for this picture of human misery." But if he speaks of the growth of American culture
in this century, he will undoubtedly point to the picture
of the American college girl, and he will say: "This picture of human splendor would scarcely have arisen without
the achievements of European culture." Both pictures
will serve to enlighten future generations on the subject
of human failure and human endeavor.

The last act in the academic life of the college girl consists of commencement, the solemn conclusion of her study.
Here she receives her first academic degree in the presence
of her parents and brothers and sisters, her friends and
relatives, to the accompaniment of festive music and the
earnest words of farewell spoken by prominent personalities. Dressed in the academic cap and gown, she accepts
her baccalaureate degree with a modest smile and scarcely
perceptible nervousness.

Her diploma and any other distinctions she has earned
which are handed to her on this occasion she usually gives
to her father or mother while the ceremonies are still going
on. They are given and received without a word, not so
much to avoid disturbing the ceremony but because there

is little more to say once the goal has been achieved. The college girl and her parents are glad, and both know that they are glad. Why say it in so many words?

Commencement really means "the beginning." Thus the final ceremony, according to the original meaning of the term, is the beginning of a new phase of life for the graduate. Actually, she concluded her study a few days before, on the day that she passed all her required examinations. At commencement she officially says "Farewell" to the days she spent in the lovely little world of the campus; at the same time she says "hail" to the unknown future days in the great world. From now on, for the rest of her life, she will move to and fro between these two worlds. Many times in her thoughts she will say *Aufwiedersehen* to her alma mater, and many times she will return in spirit, consciously or unconsciously, for counsel and strength.

When she leaves the commencement exercises she is no longer a college girl. She is a graduate, an academic person, a young woman with a college education. Thereafter not only the designation of her rank is changed, but also her environment and her outlook. You notice the change even in her facial expression. Something like nostalgia is awakening in her psyche that embraces both, what she is leaving and what she is meeting. She becomes more serious and more thoughtful. She asks herself how she is going to find her way in life without the help of her parents and her teachers. Will she succeed in realizing the plans she made on the campus?

From the small, sheltered world the girl steps into the great world where she confronts many difficulties and in which she must convert her theoretical knowledge into practical action. She must struggle with the complexities of daily life about which she knows from hearsay but which she has yet to experience. She will not be spared disappointments and failures, for that is the fate of every mortal, even the most gifted. At such moments she will involuntarily remember those days on the campus when everything went smoothly and without friction, when, free from anxiety, she could often laugh. Then, in her thoughts, she will take refuge in her alma mater. A college chaplain once showed me the letter of a young woman who had graduated seven years before. Among other things, I read these words: "They told us that it was cold out here. Why didn't they tell us that it is freezing?"

At times, life can taste very bitter to her. But it does not make her bitter. She has learned how to take care of herself and how to help others. Besides, she is equipped to make her own living. She knows how to make good friends, and how to be content even if she is alone. And all this—the mastery of the art of life—she owes largely to her alma mater. The following statements of a few graduates bear witness to this.

An office worker writes:

"The courses taken in college opened entirely new avenues of thought and cultural development. The associations formed have materially added to my happiness. I cannot conceive that a college education could be a disappointment to anyone. If the individual believes himself to be disappointed it may be not because of the college or the courses taken but that the cause may be found within himself. He may not be college material, have chosen the wrong professional field, or be emotionally undeveloped."[22]

A teacher writes:

"Without college training, I expect that I should be something of a misanthrope or a perpetually disgruntled person, always seeking knowledge but never being quite satisfied or secure about what I gathered. It has made a tremendous impression on my life—one that I am grateful for. I don't mean to sound smug, for I don't feel that because I have been to college I am automatically a better person than my neighbor. All I know is that the academic life suits my nature, and I am glad that I was able to recognize my needs and fulfill them. That is what I believe makes me a better citizen and one who is willing to take responsibility in my community.

"College showed me the way to develop my special talents more quickly and completely than a mere high school education would have. College, however, never makes a person what he isn't. It can help the individual to broaden his potentialities, but it can't implant seed on barren ground and one cannot expect to reap a full harvest solely because the seed was sown."[23]

From a housewife:

"My college training has given me a sense of accomplishment, a broadening of viewpoint, a feeling of being able to evaluate situations that arise and material that may come to my attention. I don't know how college could have helped me more."[24]

The college girl as a composite of the elite of young American women of the last half century is somewhat different from the Gibson Girl (the magazine-cover-girl of the pre-World War I years) despite the fact that she is "immaculate and bewitching"[25] as the latter was. Nor has she much in common with the American girls of the nineties, "made up as Sweet Rosie O'Grady or Mamie O'Rourke," despite the fact that she is also merry and gay as they were. She is neither "definitely high life" nor "definitely low life." And how different she is from "the short-haired, short-skirted hoyden of the twenties, . . . something of caricature to begin with."

The college girl is rather a happy composite of "definitely high life" and "definitely low life," a moderately full life. If you want to know what is proper and what is improper, you will ask her because you sense that she will give you the proper advice in a delightful way.[26] At the same time she is one with whom you may jest without hesitation, for you have the feeling that she will respond in a friendly manner, that she is a type who would join you "in stealing horses" (German folk saying).

It is her cultivated taste in work and play that distinguishes her even when she is "short-haired" and "short-skirted." And it is precisely because of that—because of her college education, to put it in a simple way—that she is, as a graduate, able to master life with a sense of delight and wisdom. Her neighbors will be surprised to learn, how much they mean to her. Therefore, she will grow in joy by giving joy without even sensing what a blessing she is for her country and for mankind.

Experiences and sacrifices will purify her sense of delight and wisdom. Finally, she may come to realize that her intellectual, social and aesthetic pursuits are but bridges leading to the new perceptions of the old realities: the truth that we are able to prove is obscure, and the Truth that we are unable to prove is clear; the man we know is imperfect, and the One we don't know is perfect; the beauty we see is little, and the Beauty we cannot see is great.

With this comprehension she enters a new dimension of her life, where the fear to die scarcely exists any more.

The campus where the American college girl spends her time is not, as many are inclined to assume, a country-club-like setting in which to enjoy leisure, but rather a pleasant location, designed for intellectual work arranged for complete human growth. She comes here to labor with her mind and to refine her taste in an academic milieu which is both inspiring and challenging. When she leaves the campus at the end of her college education, she is a transformed person:

> beauteous (add the beauty of her mind) rather than glamorous;
> orderly rather than extravagant;
> graceful rather than dreamy;
> pensive rather than talkative;
> cautious rather than reserved;
> modest rather than shy;
> cared-for rather than spoiled;
> delightful rather than sweet;
> critical rather than naive;
> sensible rather than sensitive;
> witty rather than beatniky;
> discriminating rather than posing;
> prudent rather than sophisticated;
> considerate rather than imposing;
> co-operative rather than demanding;
> eager to help rather than to be helped;

striving for joy (including the soul's joy) rather than for a good time;

individual rather than conventional (shaped by the etiquette makers);

catholic rather than provincial-minded.

The American college girl is neither an idealist nor a realist; she is rather a mixture of both—a keen person eager to arrest that which delights and to preserve that which purifies.

Appendix: The College Girl Speaks About Herself

> *"You'll probably find yourself wondering (as I did) at the end of each year in college how it can be that you're still physically the same person who was trying so hard to make the right decision about college."*

Nannerl Overholser, Junior at Wellesley College, Wellesley, Massachusetts:

There's quite an important jump from senior year in high school to freshman year in college. The problems you have to face are different, and people expect you to solve them with more independence and maturity, all of a sudden. Everything from when to do your laundry to the choice of a major is up to you, and it's a lot of responsibility as well as a lot of new freedom. Also, there are many new advantages and opportunities involved. This all leads gradually to a greater awareness of yourself as a person and also to clearer knowledge of what other people are like.

Obviously it makes a difference whether you go to college close to home or far away, with a group of close friends or on your own, to a small college or a large university. I am only in a position to judge one sort of educational experience, but I can recommend it wholeheartedly to anyone with background and interests similar to my own. I came from a small town in the South to a top-ranking New England women's college, and perhaps this is why I emphasize the importance of the adjustment you have to make.

Most important perhaps, your intellectual life changes radically. You are no longer well-known by your teachers, consistently at the top of your class. You are Miss So-and-so, and the realization that nobody knows your family or the fact that you *always* got good grades (since everybody else did, too) makes you see that you will be judged completely on what you do as an individual. The academic life at college is so important that it would be impossible to praise it too highly. The excellence of professors, the amount of concentrated and very interesting work and reading, the stimulating conversation in class and the fascinating bull sessions in the dorm, all sharply accentuate the importance of thinking and writing, of growing in mental acuteness and depth. If this sounds good to you, then you'll enjoy it immensely and find that the periods of pressure when the requirements are really stiff (something like growing pains—they hurt, but they're necessary) are far outweighed by the deep pleasure you'll receive from developing mentally—because, after all, that's what education really is.

This concentration on and appreciation of things academic may not be so strong everywhere, so if you are interested in having it, make sure you go to a college where you can get it. This does not necessarily mean a prestige college, but it does require an excellent library, dedicated professors, and some other students around who are interested in the same thing.

In order to make this experience as meaningful as possible, it is also important, of course, that you choose a college where you will be happiest socially and emotionally. This may be more difficult to do, because you can't tell what factors will make you happy until you begin to live with them.

First of all, many of the assets and liabilities will be determined by whether it's a women's college or coeducational. Your problems will be completely different and so will many of the values.

If you like having boys around for coffee dates and casual encounters, or if you like to have them in the classroom because they have different views on things, you won't be happy in a women's college. The social aspect of life is treated in a completely different way in a women's college; during the week you can relax and wander around as absent-mindedly as you wish without fear of encountering your Saturday night date. You don't have to worry about the pressure to date during the week or in classes; but on the other hand, the emphasis on dating on Saturday night can be rather oppressive, since there aren't too many opportunities to meet boys. I would certainly recommend that you try to pick a women's college close to at least one men's college. Wellesley is wonderful in this respect with Harvard and M. I. T. and all the advantages of Boston thirty minutes away. You'll find that your chances to meet boys are limited to mixers and blind dates (unless you arrive with convenient connections at the men's college), both of which are usually rather strained situations, at least at first. But if you have any kind of luck at all, you'll find that the social side of life will soon settle into its proper perspective.

Unless you are lucky enough to go to school near a city, you'll find that your dating situations usually revolve around the fraternity party weekend, which presents some problems of a special nature. These can be great fun if you're lucky enough to be with a date you like. But if you unfortunately get stuck with a loser or a cave man type, make sure you have your wits and your sense of humor about you.

A women's college can be the best place anywhere for forming close friendships and getting to know other people well; the closeness of dormitory life is invaluable, as are even the stresses and strains involved. The more varied your acquaintances, the richer your experience will be. This is probably one of the biggest advantages of an Eastern women's college.

The atmosphere of a college is difficult to gauge from the outside, but can be extremely important to you on the inside. Clues include: size—impersonal or intimate; location—sophisticated urban or cheerful countryside; the things emphasized by the catalog; and alumnae you talk with. A visit to the campuses you are seriously considering should be a must if you can. If not, be sure to talk to any representatives they send. Remember your tastes and preferences always when you are judging, though, and try to picture yourself in reference to the things you hear.

It sounds trite, but what college will mean to you depends a great deal on what you want to get from it. If you're interested in social contacts, the advantages of city or university life, the prestige of a degree, special schools or laboratory equipment, then look at colleges with these things in mind. But make sure that you aren't controlled by a passing fancy. These things have got to be important a year, four years from now—and the rest of your life. It's also important to remember, however, that it's pretty hard to make a bad choice if you keep your eyes open, so don't be paralyzed by the importance of the decision.

To be more specific, Wellesley College has many advantages which I would like to emphasize. I have already mentioned the location—close to Boston, but completely self-contained, with beautiful lake and woods. The buildings are exceptionally lovely, and besides being a source of pride, a beautiful campus is excellent for the morale. The size allows variety in the student body and excellence of faculty, but it is not so large that you can get lost in it easily. We are decidedly casual during the week—Bermudas or skirts with crew-necks and knee socks; for weekends, the wool dress which can travel comfortably and appear at the game as well as a cocktail party is standard equipment. There is very little opportunity to show off an exceptional wardrobe. One of the best things about Wellesley is that though it may have a reputation for snobbishness, there is no consciousness of which girls have scholarships and which girls are daughters of millionaires. No one really cares—and it's a good feeling.

The structure of Wellesley's program for concentration is flexible enough so that you never feel stuck in one department; there is a great deal of emphasis on related courses. I find that a major in political science with several history, English, and philosophy courses, plus an exploration of economics, psychology, Bible and French, makes my plan of concentration varied and gives me insight into the differences and interrelationships of many fields.

College is so many things that can't come out on paper; the changes that take place in your outlook on life, in your appraisal of situations and your evaluation of other people, in your awareness of the intellectual history that has preceded you and the thinking that is going on about you, are so very important for the development of your personality that you'll probably find yourself wondering (as I did) at the end of each year in college how it can be that you're still physically the same person who was trying so hard to make the right decision about college. Can it be only three years ago?[27]

Jeanne Von Kamen, Junior at College Misericordia, Dallas, Pennsylvania:

Autumn comes slowly and deliberately to northeastern Pennsylvania and the campus of College Misericordia. The deep, plush greens of summer melt almost imperceptibly into the pale reds and lemon yellows of late September. August's flowers give place one by one, and with deceiving ease, to the blossoms of fall. Then suddenly, as an eager young ruler makes full use of newly acquired authority, October asserts itself, and overnight appear the crimsons and the scarlets, the saffron and the gold, and the fire-shades.

Not unlike this seasonal progression is the life of a Misericordian, who begins her college career on a note of hope which grows through four years from its symbolic green to the fall-gold splendor of personal fulfillment. The life of a Misericordia student, as of any college woman, is neither the romantic ideal flaunted by writers of teenage novels, nor the life of ease fabricated by a few cynical critics; very often, in fact, the "fall-gold splendor" is entirely subconscious—shaded or buried by practical problems and conflicts. But always it is there, a driving force to success at work and play.

Freshman Investiture, set against the russet and gold tones of the campus' mid-October background, represents the acceptance by the entering class of all the intellectual, spiritual, aesthetic, social, and physical aspects of college life. The impressive ceremony holds meaning, however, for upperclassmen as well, and the oak leaves which each student carries in procession symbolize the pledge of loyalty which she and her school are exchanging.

But it is not during ceremonies, primarily, that loyalty is put to work; rather it is in the classroom where the student learns for the sake of learning; where she proves an argument of her own to be right, or succumbs to the more logical arguments of teacher or classmate; it is in dormitories or at class meetings where she plans activities with others, and puts her talents to work to accomplish them; it is over coffee and cherry pie at the local haunt—in Misericordia's case, Dixon's Restaurant, "in the heart of Dallas"—where she discusses decorations for the Sophomore Cotillion, or the value of visual aids in elementary education.

As loyalty cannot be localized, neither can intellectual pursuit be confined to the classroom. Snatches of conversation in College Misericordia's lounge, smoker, cafeteria, or halls reveal dynamic interest in the immediate causes of the Fall of Troy or in William Butler Yeats's mythological allusions. Saturday afternoon in McAuley Hall is likely to find six or seven sophomores (three bathrobe clad, books or knitting needles in hands, two or three in sweaters and skirts, perhaps one in raincoat and heels, ready for a trip to Wilkes-Barre) discussing a variety of topics, from Bach to the advisability of a course in modern algebra. Not that lounge or dorm conversations always center on intellectual subjects, for such is not the case. The same who talk of Troy and Yeats, and Bach and math, talk also of "Sunset Strip" and Ogden Nash, Ray Conniff and riddles. And so it should be!

Misericordia is a Catholic college, conducted by the Religious Sisters of Mercy. As a religiously affiliated institution, its atmosphere is naturally pervasively spiritual. Through the daily offering of the Mass, the recitation of the rosary nightly, and various curricular and extracurricular functions, it furnishes ample opportunity for its students' spiritual development. In the classroom and out, College Misericordia aims to provide a liberal education: to educate the individual toward the development of *all* his powers.

If there is a symbol of spirituality, or of goodness, at Misericordia, it is the postulants and novices of the Mercy Order. (The Dallas campus includes, in addition to the college, the Mother House and novitiate of the Sisters of Mercy.) These young nuns, some of them as the youngest of the college girls, are a ceaseless source of wonder and inspiration. The professed Sisters are in closer contact with the students: they are teachers and housemothers, club and class moderators—respected, admired, liked, and too often taken for granted. But the postulants and novices —those who clap so loudly and enthusiastically at piano concerts, and walk so quietly and serenely into chapel; who speak thoughtful words in the classroom, and welcome with coaxing tenderness a stray and hungry dog; whose voices squeal with delight over snowmen or snowballs, and ring with a sweetness bordering on the celestial as they sing Benediction—they remain ever a novelty!

To the precious stone of intellectual and spiritual growth College Misericordia adds the polished lustre of aesthetic appreciation. Through piano, string, and vocal concerts (classical and popular, given by professional musicians or members of the college's Music Department); through courses in music and art appreciation, and use of a library well equipped for listening as well as reading; through lectures and discussions on literature and world affairs, and through the annual presentation of three professional performances of cultural spectacles (Theatre Three, a project sponsored by the college for the community's as well as its own benefit), the student finds the opportunity, and often the enthusiasm, to develop her own sense of the beautiful.

At every women's college there are laments that social opportunities—of the boy-girl variety, that is—are severely limited. But there are also cries, usually equal in number if not in volume and intensity, of the Saturday night date, the crowded prom, the fraternity pin, the engagement ring, which testify to the existence of many happy relationships. At its worst the situation is not without its advantages. The student of a women's college is less apt than the coed to be accused of seeking an education solely to find a husband!

Apart from this controversial aspect of the college student's social progress, but as important, are relationships with fellow students, professors, the world at large. A student must learn to hold her own not only in her business or professional life, but in her society, her world. This she does learn at Misericordia by developing stable, healthy relationships with others, be they contemporaries, elders, or the children for whom she babysits or student teaches. If she is a resident student, perhaps her roommate is her biggest asset, and her unwitting instructor in this vital lesson. For living so close to a person who is at first a stranger, but whom she comes to know better perhaps than her own sister, is indeed a maturing experience. Not that the "fall-gold splendor" is here always conscious; but after all, "conscious splendor" could become very monotonous. In learning to give up—to sacrifice for friendship's sake —some of the things she wants, she finds what actually she wants more: an education in the art of living.

Through club and other group activities, the Misericordian finds an outlet for excess mental and physical energy. She may read a research paper to an English seminar, or practice with the varsity basketball team; play in the orchestra, or walk in the beautiful May Day procession; participate in an education club panel discussion, sing in the glee club, or just stroll the campus. But always she is learning.

Yes, autumn comes slowly and deliberately to northeastern Pennsylvania and the campus of College Misericordia; and another autumn, and another, and still another come during the college career of a Misericordia student. Soon the years which many tell her are the best of her life are gone. Perhaps for their youthful fun and idealism they will, in retrospect, be the best; but more likely they will be merely a preparation for better years, for a truly profitable life on earth, and for eternity—for an education in the truest sense of the word.[28]

Reference Notes

1 (p. 14)   First written in German and published in Coburg in 1950, under the title *Porträt des Heimatlosen;* the enlarged English edition, entitled *The Refugee,* with a preface by Pitirim A. Sorokin, appeared in Boston in 1957.

2 (p. 18)   "College is the setting for the most elaborate social life available to young people in our society. There is no comparable publicity or promise of gaiety connected with any other life period. The wedding day is the only other symbol of equal splendor, and this has much more solemn overtones." —Elizabeth M. Douvan, "Adolescent Girls: Their Attitudes toward Education," in: Opal D. David, ed.: *The Education of Women—Signs for the Future* (American Council on Education, Washington, 1959), p. 26.

3 (p. 19)   "Agnes Scott College points out that since it admits very few students each year—only 180—it must have a highly selective program. The college comments, in describing the underlying policies used in choosing these girls: 'We like them to be bright, well-prepared, pretty and competent.' "— Benjamin Fine, *Admission to American Colleges. A Study of Current Policy and Practice* (New York, 1946), p. 193.

4 (p. 19)   "Most application blanks have a space in which the petitioner may inscribe his or her reasons for especially desiring admission to Insert-Name-of-College, but few attain

the clarity, candor and brevity of the girl who wrote, 'I wish to come to Mills to be with horses.' (She was admitted and turned out to have more than equestrian talents.)"—Lynn White, Jr., *Educating Our Daughters* (New York, 1950), p. 141.

5 (p. 33) One may wonder, knowing how realistic and practical they are, "Do they have dreams and yearnings?" Certainly, they have affectionate dreams and romantic yearnings, only they show them less than the youths of the past.

6 (p. 46) "The woman's ever-present pressure to attract and please men is never more self-conscious than in her campus years, and it very much affects her classroom and extra-classroom behavior."—Kate Hevner Mueller, "The Cultural Pressures on Women," in: Opal D. David, ed., op. cit., p. 50.

7 (p. 57) "But stop one in the rain and ask for directions, and she will smile and patiently explain the way, showing those marvelous teeth which seem to gleam brighter at Smith than anywhere else."—David Boroff, "Smith: A College for ARG's with High IQ's," in: *Mademoiselle,* March 1961, p. 125.

8 (p. 61) Vergil, *Aeneid,* I, 490-493.

9 (p. 61) Ibid., VII, 807.

10 (p. 69) A sophomore from Sarah Lawrence College confesses: "Concerning my courses, I consider a few general ideas I got from them more important than any specific experiences; the Comic Spirit in Literature taught me to really think of what humor is, to try to analyze it, and to see more clearly than ever the importance of laughter; from German I learned more about the complexity of the English language; in Mathematics the idea of infinity was most thought-provoking, and gave me a better perspective on the greatness and smallness of things human and material. . . . I learned . . . that during the death march on Bataan, the men put pebbles into their mouths to keep from being thirsty, and thus resisted drinking polluted water; that the first firing of gunpowder was as frightening to its contemporaries as the atomic bomb is to us; that it is impossible for an educated person with any conscience, common sense, and perspective

to try to go his own way and ignore the rest of the world."
—Lois B. Murphy and Esther Rauschenbusch, eds., *Achieve-
ment in the College Years. A Record of Intellectual and
Personal Growth* (New York, 1960), pp. 97-98.

11 (p. 71)   " 'If the assignment sheet has a "typo" and calls
for 300 pages overnight instead of 30, they'll do it,' a government professor said."—David Boroff, op. cit., p. 182.

12 (p. 71)   The will to work hard eliminates her emotional
problems and helps her to maintain her mental stability. If
she runs, however, into serious emotional troubles, there is
always available to her a religious custodian or a psychiatrist.
In fact, she needs either of them only seldom; the academic
milieu protects her from excesses. (If she has to struggle with
the so-called "identity crisis," especially in her first college
year, she copes with it, as a rule, in the spirit of a challenge
rather than despair.)

13 (p. 76)   "The educational features of the extracurricular
program are many. Those most frequently mentioned are (1)
religious training; (2) a manual-work program; (3) a college
lecture and concert program; (4) training in "behavior be-
fitting a gentleman or a lady"; (5) student government;
(6) student-initiated activities; and (7) the opportunity to
associate informally with other intelligent and educated
people, whether students or faculty. All these have been
consciously fostered by one or another residential college as
factors contributing to the end product—a well-rounded personality."—Mabel Newcomer, *A Century of Higher Education for American Women* (New York, 1959), p. 107.

14 (p. 98)   Ernest Havemann and Patricia Salter West, *They
Went to College* (New York, 1952), p. 78.

15 (p. 116)   A different opinion is expressed by Sister Mary
Denise, R.S.M., Head of the English Department at College
Misericordia, in a letter to the author: "Some of the most
cultivated and, ultimately, the most successful students I
have had, worked their way through and received hindrance
rather than help from home. Resident students, having everything handed to them, so to speak, often waste their time

in frivolity. I would not say, of course, that this is the rule; only that it is common."

16 (p. 119) A graduate of Vassar College states: "I think more serious work can be and is done in a noncoëd college. We concentrated on studying in large doses during the week and our social life was intensive on weekends."—Ernest Havemann and Patricia Salter West, op. cit., p. 217.

17 (p. 120) "The separate education of women has as its prime virtue the accomplishment of a sense of identity by the individual about herself. There is a certain privacy and a possibility for personal growth for the woman student in a women's college. If the conditions are congenial to growth, the factor of privacy is an important one in allowing the student to become herself before she is impelled to adapt her own character and personality to the demands placed on her by a men's society."—Harold Taylor, "Liberal Thought and the Women's College," in: Opal D. David, ed., op. cit., p. 85.

18 (p. 122) "In conclusion, the average college woman today appears to be a better wife and mother, a better housekeeper, and a more active and better community worker than the average noncollege woman."—Mabel Newcomer, op. cit., p. 231.

19 (p. 150) *"Comme Christophe Colombe quand il se mit à la voile,/Sa pensée n'était pas de trouver une terre nouvelle, /Mais dans ce coeur plein de sagesse la passion de la limite et de la sphère calculée de parfaire l'éternel horizon."*—Paul Claudel, *Cinq Grandes Odes* (Paris 1936), p. 143.

20 (p. 168) If one learns that in American public high schools the "A" student, not the "F" student, is considered a hero by his fellow students, if one meets an American housewife who prefers reading a book by Plato to watching "soap-operas" on TV, if one reads in newspapers about an American movie star who sincerely doesn't believe in divorce, one is inclined to think about the emerging image of an unAmerican American, the American way of life of tomorrow.

21 (p. 169) "We Americans must again commit ourselves to great ends. We must resume our searching, surging, questing.

Then, assuredly, we will come nearer the vision of John Adams of Massachusetts, who, in 1813, assured his friend Thomas Jefferson that our republic would some day 'introduce the perfection of man.' "—John F. Kennedy, "We Must Climb to the Hilltop," in: *Life*, August 22, 1960, pp. 70-72.

22 (p. 173)   Ernest Havemann and Patricia Salter West, op. cit., p. 134.

23 (p. 174)   Ibid., p. 134.

24 (p. 174)   Ibid., p. 136.

25 (p. 175)   This phrase and the subsequent phrases are from the article "The Gibson Girl" by Agnes Rogers, in: *American Heritage*, December 1957, p. 98.

26 (p. 175)   *"Willst du genau erfahren, was sich ziemt, so frage nur bei edlen Frauen an."*—Goethe, *Torquato Tasso*.

27 (p. 183)   Reprinted from the *Bulletin of Wellesley College*, Vol. 49, No. 6, April 1960, with the permission of the Director of Publicity of Wellesley College.

28 (p. 187)   This paper was written at the author's request.